C. PRITCHARD

Senior Lecturer in Geography
Environmental Studies Department
Bordesley College of Education, Birmingham

The West Midlands

CONTENTS

GEOGRAPHY OF THE BRITISH ISLES SERIES
GENERAL EDITOR: A. V. HARDY

CAMBRIDGE UNIVERSITY PRESS

Published by the Syndics of the Cambridge University Press
Bentley House, 200 Euston Road, London NW1 2DB

© Cambridge University Press 1974

ISBN: 0 521 20029 6
First published 1974

Photoset and printed in Malta by St Paul's Press Ltd

Geography of the British Isles Series

Wales   H. J. SAVORY
Greater London   W. S. DANCER AND A. V. HARDY
North West England   W. E. MARSDEN
Yorkshire and North Lincolnshire   H. TOLLEY AND K. ORRELL
South-East England   H. J. SAVORY
North East England   J. E. WALTHAM AND W. D. HOLMES
Northern Ireland   D. A. HILL
The West Midlands   C. PRITCHARD

ACKNOWLEDGEMENTS

Thanks are due to the following people and organisations for supplying illustrations or information on which illustrations have been based:

Dr C. H. Sands for Figs. 2.2, 2.4, 8.1; Tarmac Roadstone Holdings Ltd for Figs. 2.5, 2.6; Aerofilms Ltd for Figs. 3.1, 4.4, 4.7, 5.1, 9.8, 10.3, 10.5; H.M.S.O. for Figs. 2.3, 3.5, 3.9, 4.1, 4.2, 4.8, 6.8, 7.2, 7.8, 8.9, 9.5, 9.7, 9.15, 10.1; P. Baker for Fig. 3.6, Public Works Department, City of Birmingham Corporation for Figs. 4.3, 4.6, 4.17, 4.1 (table); Midlands New Town Society for Fig. 4.9; Droitwich Town Development for Fig. 4.10; Telford Development Corporation for Figs. 4.11, 4.12, 4.13; Redditch Development Corporation for Figs. 4.14, 4.15, 4.16; Architects Department, City of Birmingham Corporation for Figs. 5.5, 5.6, 5.7, 5.8; Victoria County History Warwickshire VII p. 41 for Fig. 5.9; British Rail for Figs. 5.10, 5.12, 5.13; by courtesy of Freightliners Ltd, Fig. 5.11; by courtesy of *The Birmingham Post*, Figs. 3.7, 5.14, 5.17, 11.3; Geographia Ltd for Fig. 5.15; The Ministry of Labour for Figs. 6.1, 7.3, 9.3, 10.8, 10.9; A. Westwood, Assay Master, Birmingham for Fig. 6.4; Cadbury-Schweppes Ltd for Fig. 6.7; British Leyland for Fig. 6.9; Lithograve for Fig. 6.10; County Borough of Dudley for Fig. 7.1; Coneygre Foundry, Tipton for Fig. 7.2; National Coal Board for Fig. 8.2; Central Electricity Generating Board, Midlands Region for Figs. 8.3, 8.4; West Midlands Gas Board for Figs. 8.5, 8.6; by courtesy of the *Sunday Mercury*, Birmingham; British Petroleum Company Ltd for Fig. 8.8; City of Coventry Museum for Fig. 9.1; Coventry Corporation for Figs. 9.6, 9.14, 9.16 and 9.4 (photographer Vivian Levett); Coventry Cathedral for Fig. 9.11; Charles Hansom for Fig. 9.12; Avoncroft Museum of Buildings, Bromsgrove, Worcs. for Fig. 9.13; Barlow Stanley for Fig. 10.2; J. Cole, Director, National Exhibition Centre Ltd for Fig. 11.4. Front cover pictures by courtesy of British Leyland, and the *Birmingham Post and Mail.*

1 | INTRODUCTION

In the West Midlands there are hills and valleys, old and new rocks, large cities and small villages. It is an area of variety which is changing so rapidly that it gives endless opportunities for all kinds of exploration and excursions. Fig. 1.1 covers the area we are concerned with in this book. Within the limits set by the Rivers Trent, Severn and Avon lies an upland over 400 feet (122 m) high known as the Birmingham or Midland Plateau. The valleys of the Rivers Blythe and Tame divide this upland into two:

A. A plateau stretching from the Trent valley southwards for 40 miles (64 km).
B. The East Warwickshire Plateau.

The highest part of A is a ridge of hills on the south-western edge. This forms a prominent landscape feature and is the meeting place of the City of Birmingham, the Black Country and the Green Belt.

The East Warwickshire Plateau (B) is smaller, never rising much over 600 feet (183 m) above sea level and forming less of a landmark.

Quite in contrast is the low-lying land between A and B. Draining into this from the two plateaux are many streams and rivers, the largest of which are the Rivers Blythe and Tame. These unite on a wide flood plain. The Tame, swollen by the Blythe, turns northwards, meandering across a flat valley until it meets the River Trent some 16 miles (26 km) away.

Birmingham, the second city of Great Britain, spreads over much of A (Fig. 1.1) and its influence extends over the whole of the West Midlands. In the north-west it merges with a group of industrial boroughs, Wolverhampton, Walsall, West Bromwich, Warley and Dudley, and several small towns, to form a continuous built-up area over 20 miles (32 km) wide. This we call a conurbation.

The Rivers Trent and Avon have broad valleys cut into pebble beds and soft clay. The River Severn for much of its course runs in a narrower valley over more resistant rocks. Flooding is a problem when the rivers rise after heavy rain. Fortunately gravel terraces provide dry level sites for market towns and villages. The valleys are the farming lands which supply the conurbation with milk, fresh vegetables, fruit and meat.

In the Midland plateaux and surrounding valleys about four million people live. Out of this total, over two and a half million are in the narrow industrial belt of Birmingham and the adjoining towns.

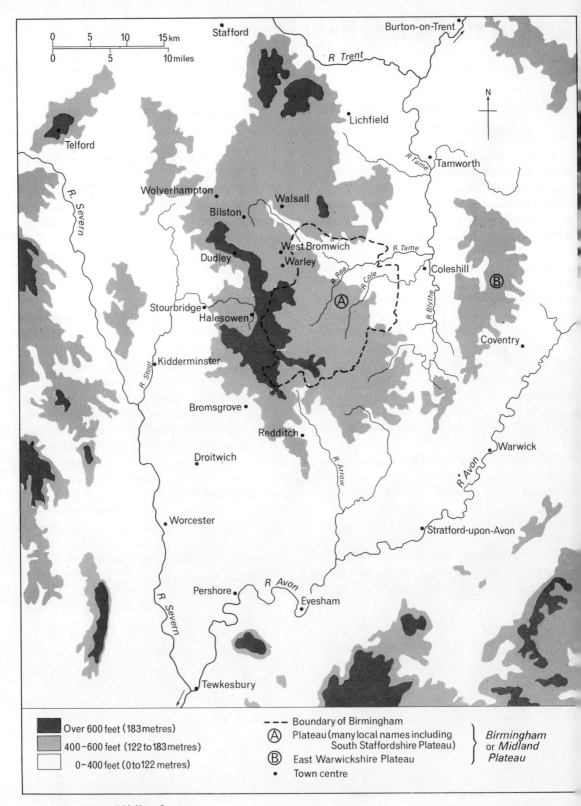

Stafford

Burton-on-Trent

R Trent

Lichfield

Telford

R Tame

Tamworth

Wolverhampton

Walsall

Bilston

West Bromwich

R Tame

Coleshill

Dudley

Warley

R Rea

R Cole

Ⓐ

Ⓑ

Stourbridge

R Blythe

Halesowen

Coventry

Kidderminster

R Stour

Bromsgrove

Redditch

Warwick

Droitwich

R Arrow

R Avon

Worcester

Stratford-upon-Avon

R Avon

Pershore

Evesham

R Severn

Tewkesbury

R. Severn

0   5   10   15 km
0   5   10 miles

N

■ Over 600 feet (183 metres)

▦ 400–600 feet (122 to 183 metres)

□ 0–400 feet (0 to 122 metres)

– – – Boundary of Birmingham

Ⓐ Plateau (many local names including
     South Staffordshire Plateau)

Ⓑ East Warwickshire Plateau

Birmingham
or *Midland
Plateau*

• Town centre

1.1 The West Midlands

2 | THE RIDGE

The highest part of the Birmingham Plateau lies to the west of Birmingham, stretching for 16 miles (26 km) from north to south as a Ridge of land rising from 600 feet above sea level to 1,036 feet (183 to 315 m). The highest points are the hills which are named on Fig. 2.1. Muck-

2.1 High points of the Ridge

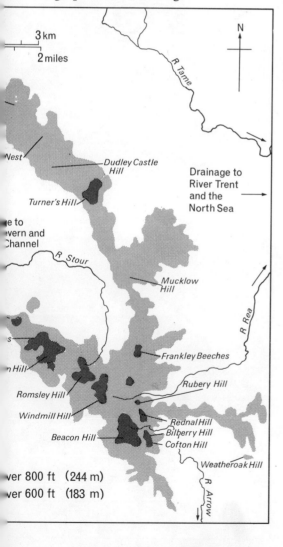

low Hill divides this Ridge into two quite different parts:

(a) The north, forming a spine running through the South Staffordshire coalfield, clustered with factories and houses, quarries and derelict workings.

(b) The south, a stretch of open park and woodland fringed by small farms.

(a) The North

The northern-most hills are Sedgley Beacon, the Wren's Nest with Mons Hill, and Dudley Castle Hill. By boarding a bus number 125, 126 or 196 at the depot in the Bull Ring Centre, Birmingham, you can go to these hills and hunt for fossils like those in the illustrations (Fig. 2.2). These fossils are the hard parts of sea animals which lived about 350 to 400 million years ago. Their broken remains formed a sediment on the sea bed, hardening into a rock called limestone. In the last 300 years men have dug out this limestone to burn for lime and to use in the iron industry. On the Wren's Nest the old workings can be dangerous, so, to help you search for fossils, a geological trail has been marked out by bollards. An excellent booklet, *Wren's Nest, Nature Reserve*, published by the Nature Conservancy, gives a map of the trail and the story of the rocks. Follow the trail to find some of the commoner fossils (Fig. 2.2), but remember that a complete trilobite is a rare find.

Limestone is no longer quarried and the hills are riddled with pits and tunnels from which the rock was taken. The Zoo in the grounds of Dudley Castle uses some of the old pits as attractive animal enclosures.

The Ridge continues south to Turner's Hill, Fig. 2.3, where there are working quarries of dolerite. This rock is quite different from limestone and originated in the interior of the earth. Moving rather like hot treacle, the molten rock or magma forced its way up into layers of rock

5

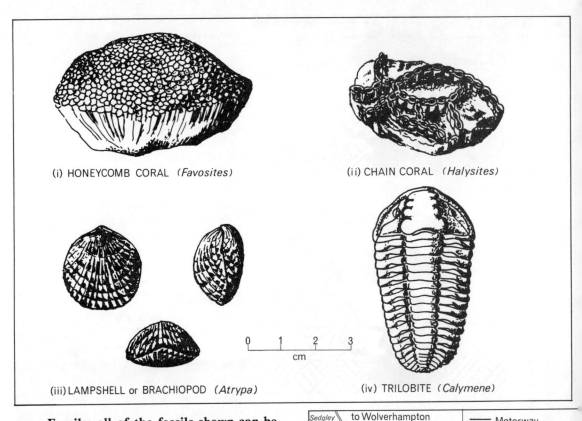

(i) HONEYCOMB CORAL (*Favosites*)

(ii) CHAIN CORAL (*Halysites*)

(iii) LAMPSHELL or BRACHIOPOD (*Atrypa*)

(iv) TRILOBITE (*Calymene*)

2.2 Fossils: all of the fossils shown can be found in the Silurian rocks of the Dudley area. The two corals shown are colonial forms; the specimen of chain coral (ii) has been etched from the rock to show the way in which the colony is built up from many tubular individuals. Three views of the Lampshell are given so that its shape may be appreciated. *Calymene*, the trilobite (iv), is a relatively common species in the Silurian of the Midlands.

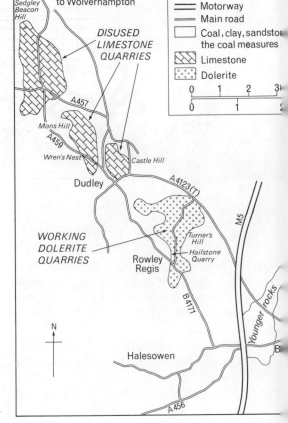

2.3 Geological sketch-map of the northern part of the Ridge (based on 1″ sheets 167 and 168 (solid) of the Geological Survey)

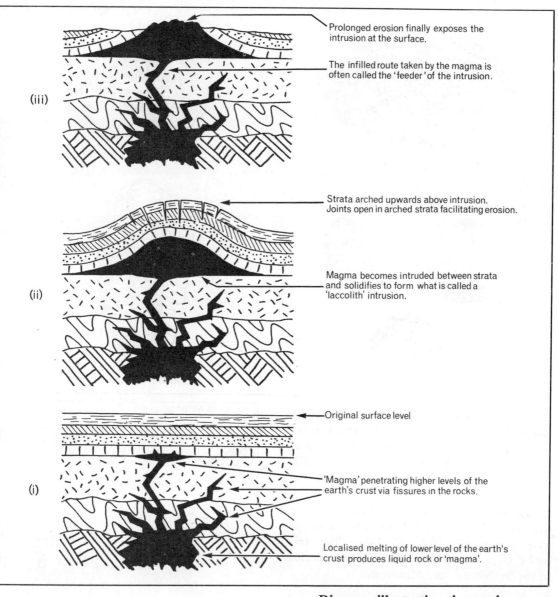

(iii) Prolonged erosion finally exposes the intrusion at the surface.

The infilled route taken by the magma is often called the 'feeder' of the intrusion.

(ii) Strata arched upwards above intrusion. Joints open in arched strata facilitating erosion.

Magma becomes intruded between strata and solidifies to form what is called a 'laccolith' intrusion.

(i) Original surface level

'Magma' penetrating higher levels of the earth's crust via fissures in the rocks.

Localised melting of lower level of the earth's crust produces liquid rock or 'magma'.

2.4 Diagram illustrating the emplacement of the dolerite intrusion at Turner's Hill (not to scale)

near the earth's surface. This happened some 280 million years ago. Since then the top rocks have worn away and the dolerite lies on the surface. The diagrams, Fig. 2.4, will help you to understand this.

Dolerite is very hard and durable. For hundreds of years rock has been taken from Turner's Hill to be used for walls, buildings and roads. Today the motorways and roads being con-structed all over the West Midlands demand huge quantities of roadstone. Hailstone Quarry, Fig. 2.5, is one of five owned by Tarmac Roadstone Ltd in the Rowley Regis area. The rock is blasted from the quarry face, crushed into 6-inch (15-cm) and then 3-inch (7.5-cm) pieces, when it is suitable for use as roadstone. Some is crushed still finer and mixed with tar. Tar-coated stone is used for surfacing roads. It can be spread cold and is

7

known as macadam. A finer tar-coated stone called asphalt is loaded into lorries whilst still hot and taken immediately to the road or footpath to be spread, rolled and left to harden. Quite likely, you have seen both kinds of road surfaces being laid. The Tarmac Group has over fifty manufacturing plants such as this in England, Wales and Scotland. The asphalt and macadam are not transported more than 40 miles (64 km) from a plant, so each serves its own region. Between Turner's Hill and the east and south coasts of England there is no other workable outcrop of dolerite. So the quarries on the Ridge hold a key position for supplying roadstone to plants in south-east England.

(b) The South

The southern part of the ridge is formed by two lines of hills:

1. The Lickey Hills, which are Rubery, Rednal, Bilberry, Cofton, Beacon.
2. The Clent Hills, which are Wychbury, Walton, Romsley, Windmill.

On the day of the coronation of Queen Elizabeth II, a fire was lit on Beacon Hill. This was a celeb-

ration, but in earlier times a fire was a signal of danger, a way of sending a message through the countryside. Beacon Hill is nearly 1,000 feet (306 m) high and from the top on a clear day Sugar Loaf Mountain, 57 miles (92 km) away in South Wales, is visible on the skyline. The Lickey Hills are covered with open parkland, a large part being a gift from the Cadbury family, whose chocolate factory is at Bournville, not far away.

The narrow lanes of the Clent Hills are popular with motorists, and on the hill tracks horse-riders compete with walkers. The National Trust owns a considerable area there. It is possible that a part of the Clent Hills may become a Country Park which people will be able to visit for recreation; parking, picnic sites and long-distance footpaths would be provided.

The Lickey and Clent Hills are mainly composed of sandstone, breccia and pebble beds, more recent rocks than those in the northern part of the Ridge. The sandy soils support gorse, bracken and trees. There are some sand quarries, and the pebble beds are quarried for gravel. There is, however, one important older rock, called quartzite. This is brought to the surface in the Lickey

Hills by faulting. It is a hard resistant rock extensively quarried for roadstone.

If the towns on or near the Ridge are mapped as in Fig. 2.7, it will be seen that there are many more in the north than in the south. Why is this? Look again at the map, and you will notice that most of the towns lie on a coalfield. A rich coal seam 30 feet (9.2 m) thick outcropped at the surface over wide areas. Associated with some of the coal seams were iron ore and fireclay. In the nineteenth century large numbers of workers moved into this district to mine the coal or to work in the blast furnaces. Bricks for lining the furnaces could be made from fireclay, and coal in the form of coke was used for smelting the iron ore and limestone. The many furnaces and foundries in which the iron was smelted and forged belched forth much smoke and fumes. These blackened the buildings and countryside and the area became known as the Black Country.

The villages grew rapidly into towns; Wednesbury, Dudley, Tipton, West Bromwich, Darlaston and Willenhall were important centres of the iron industry. On the south-west of the coalfield, nail-making became concentrated in Stourbridge,

Lye, Halesowen, Brierley Hill and Netherton. Today the coal, iron ore and limestone deposits are either worked out or too costly to obtain. In spite of this, the towns are still important centres of the metal industry. Industrial towns did not develop further south because there is no coalfield in the southern part of the Ridge, but the villages on the eastern side have been swallowed up by the growth of the City of Birmingham.

One clear windy day I drove along the Ridge from end to end, stopping on the way at Frankley Beeches. From this hilltop, 840 feet (256 m) above sea level, I could see the City Centre of Birmingham, and sketched the main landmarks shown in Fig. 2.8. Immediately below me were farms with fields which ran down to two reservoirs served by a pipeline bringing water from Wales and the River Severn. After being filtered the water is led through pipes to supply Birmingham. With fieldglasses I picked out a dark church spire amongst the tall buildings on the skyline. This was St Martin's Church in the Bull Ring, close to the original site of Birmingham. The City has expanded so much that it now reaches to just below Frankley Beeches, that is, on to the eastern flank of the Ridge.

2.5 (*opposite page*) **Hailstone Quarry, Turner's Hill, Rowley Regis**

2.6 **Key to Fig. 2.5**

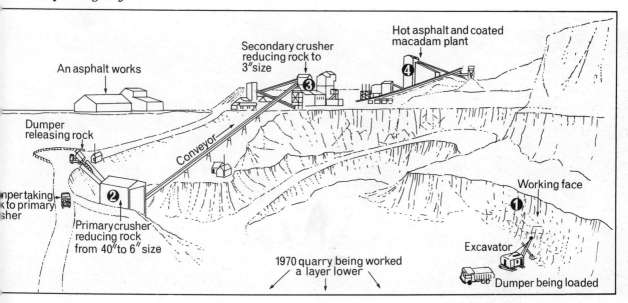

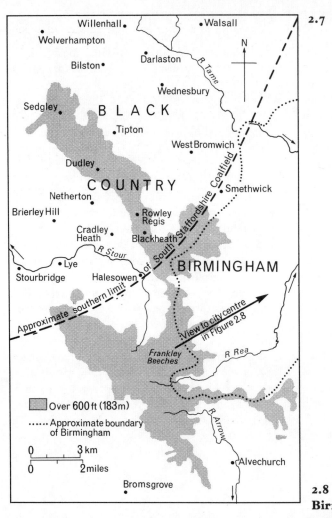

2.7 Towns on or near the Ridge

Willenhall

Walsall

Wolverhampton

Bilston

Darlaston

R Tame

N

Wednesbury

B L A C K

Sedgley

Tipton

West Bromwich

Dudley

of South Staffordshire Coalfield

C O U N T R Y

Netherton

Rowley
Regis

Smethwick

Brierley Hill

Cradley
Heath

Blackheath

BIRMINGHAM

R Stour

Lye

Stourbridge

Halesowen

View to city centre
in Figure 2.8

Approximate southern limit

Frankley
Beeches

R Rea

▨ Over 600 ft (183m)

······ Approximate boundary
of Birmingham

0   3 km

0   2 miles

R Arrow

Alvechurch

Bromsgrove

2.8 Sketch from Frankley Beeches to Birmingham City Centre

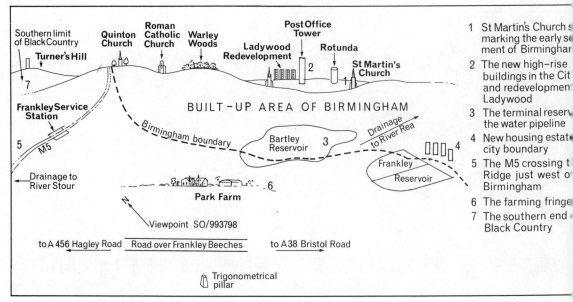

Southern limit
of Black Country

Turner's Hill

**Quinton
Church**

**Roman
Catholic
Church**

**Warley
Woods**

**Ladywood
Redevelopment**

**Post Office
Tower**

Rotunda

**St Martin's
Church**

7

2

**Frankley Service
Station**

BUILT-UP AREA OF BIRMINGHAM

5   M5

Birmingham boundary

Bartley
Reservoir

3

Drainage
to River Rea

Frankley
Reservoir

4

Drainage to
River Stour

Park Farm

6

N

Viewpoint SO/993798

to A 456 Hagley Road   Road over Frankley Beeches   to A 38 Bristol Road

⛫ Trigonometrical
pillar

1 St Martin's Church s[...]
marking the early se[...]
ment of Birmingham

2 The new high-rise
buildings in the Cit[...]
and redevelopmen[...]
Ladywood

3 The terminal reserv[...]
the water pipeline

4 New housing estat[...]
city boundary

5 The M5 crossing t[...]
Ridge just west o[...]
Birmingham

6 The farming fringe

7 The southern end [...]
Black Country

Exercises.   1. The Ridge is part of the main watershed of England. What is a watershed?
From Fig. 1.1 name the rivers which the Stour and Tame join. Use an atlas map and find out where these enter the sea. The River Arrow also rises on the Ridge. Of which river is it a tributary?

2. Name three kinds of rock found in the Ridge. Which one is worked at present? Refer to Fig. 2.6 and explain how the stone for tarmac is obtained.

3. The intrusion at Turner's Hill is a laccolith. What does this mean? What other kinds of volcanic intrusions are there?

4. Why is the north of the Ridge more industrial than the south?

5. Use the O.S. extracts (Maps B.1 and B.2) and write down what you locate at the following grid references: 968887, 946907. Name the river in square (a) 9485, (b) 0691. The ‡ at the 073866 is St Martin's Church, Birmingham; from Fig. 2.8 work out in which direction this lies from Frankley Beeches.

3 | BIRMINGHAM CITY CENTRE

3.1   Aerial view of Central Birmingham, 5 May 1964

We have seen that associated with the Ridge are many towns, including the City of Birmingham. Let us look for a moment at a recent aerial photograph of the Centre of Birmingham (Fig. 3.1). The church spire in the foreground is St Martin's Church, which I could see from the Frankley Beeches viewpoint. This stands on or near the site of a Saxon village. Records tell us that at Domesday in 1086 there was a manor house here and we know that parts of the church date back to the twelfth century. The settlement was on a dry sandstone slope overlooking the marshy valley of the River Rea. Because the Rea could be forded and later bridged at this point, the settlement was well placed. For over a thousand years people

have been walking up from the river, following much the same route as the modern road running to the right of the church. This leads to the Bull Ring, where in front of the church a weekly market has been held by charter from King Henry II since 1166.

Gradually buildings spread up the slope from St Martin's Church to flatter land where a second important part of the town developed. This was around St Philip's Church, built in 1710, which later became the cathedral. By the beginning of this century, the town hall, council house, railway stations and markets had been built within a half-mile radius of these two churches. Fig. 3.2 is a sketch to help you locate some of these buildings on the photograph.

The most striking modern building is the white round office block. This is the Rotunda, a landmark in the City Centre which has become a million, was built to keep the through traffic out of the City Centre. To do this, major routes were led into the ring road at intersections called circuses. St Martin's Circus, which shows up clearly below the Rotunda on Fig. 3.1, was the first to be completed, and you can see how the old route passing St Martin's Church feeds into it.

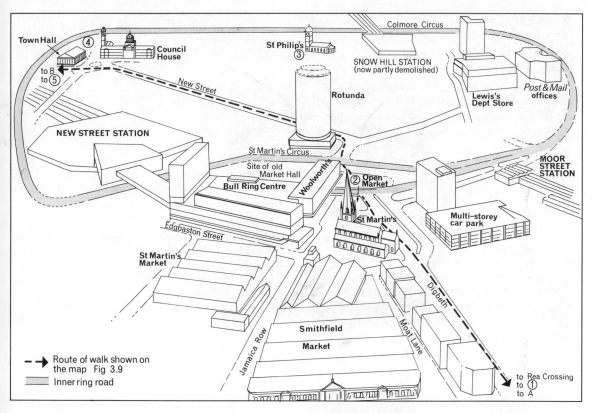

symbol of the new Birmingham, for the city is rapidly being rebuilt. The tall concrete and glass buildings are department stores, offices, banks, car parks; there will soon be little left of Victorian Birmingham in the City Centre.

Between St Martin's Church and the new Rotunda lies a ring road opened in 1971 by Queen Elizabeth II. Except for the cutting of Corporation Street in 1878, the early street pattern remained with few changes until the 1960s. Roads from the north and west met roads from the south and east at the crossing of the Rea (Fig. 3.3). The little river was hidden in a brick culvert under the modern road whilst the traffic flowed in a congested bottleneck above. Surveys showed that many vehicles were passing through Birmingham without stopping. So a ring road, costing £35

3.2 Key to Fig. 3.1

The ring road was unfinished when the photograph was taken, so its route has been sketched in on Fig. 3.2. Notice that the older site around St Martin's Church is outside the ring road, whilst the later development around St Philip's Church is neatly contained inside like an island.

The older site outside the inner ring road

The market zone remains near St Martin's Church, although from time to time the actual site of a particular market has altered. In the years until the eighteenth century Birmingham grew and prospered as an important market town. Activities spread from the Bull Ring up the High Street. In one part cattle were sold, in another pigs, and so on. In this way separate markets started. Maps of the time tell us where these were. For instance, we learn from Fig. 3.4 that there was an English Cross below which people gathered to sell butter, poultry and fruit. On the other hand cattle brought on foot from Wales were sold at the Welsh Cross.

A great improvement was made with the building of covered markets. The first one was the Market Hall, built in 1835. Here produce could be bought every day, not just on market day. By the end of the nineteenth century there were two kinds of markets:

A. *Retail* – where the housewife shopped. These were the open market and the Market Hall.

B. *Wholesale* – where the shopkeeper bought in quantity. These were the Smithfield Market for vegetables, fruit and poultry, the Meat Market and the Fish Market.

Similar markets exist today. Except for part of the open market, they all lie outside the inner ring road, and their present position is shown on Fig. 3.5. Some of them are on the photograph (Fig. 3.1).

There are over 2.5 million people in the Black Country and Birmingham to be supplied with food, mainly from these markets. All produce entering and leaving the zone does so by truck and van along narrow roads built in the time of horses and carts. In all cities where market areas are in the older part, there is similar congestion. Some solve this by moving the markets to the outskirts of the town where there is more space. Birmingham is planning to keep her markets in the centre, rebuilding the whole complex to include car parks, restaurants and offices around a better road pattern linked to the inner ring road.

The *retail* markets have been redesigned. An unusual, old outside pulpit on St Martin's Church (Fig. 3.6) overlooks the new stalls in the Bull Ring open market (Fig. 3.7). Tolls are paid here by the traders, as in the twelfth century. Under a new charter, the market can be held daily and a variety of articles, not only farming produce, is sold.

The old Market Hall was damaged during the Second World War and was finally demolished in 1964. The new Corporation indoor market to replace it occupies the ground floor of an £8,000,000 multi-level shopping centre known as the Bull Ring Centre.

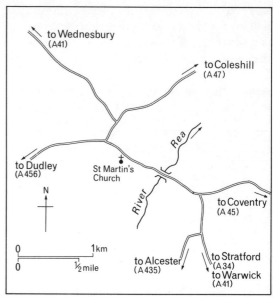

3.3 The medieval road pattern of Birmingham, with modern road classification numbers

3.4 Birmingham markets during the eighteenth century, according to contemporary maps and writings (not to scale)

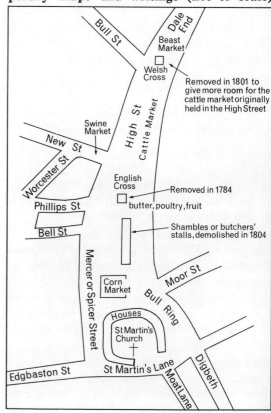

Within the dotted line in Fig. 3.5 is the *whole-sale* area. The streets are narrow and the buildings crowded together. Until recently cattle were brought daily into the abattoir to be kept overnight in lairages before slaughter and sale next day.

There is a tremendous overflow of vegetables and fruit from Smithfield and St Martin's Markets into the buildings around, used as warehouses and extra premises. At 6 a.m. the whole area is alive with people, produce, lorries, trucks and handcarts. In the Smithfield Market the traders are primary wholesalers; they obtain fruit and vegetables direct from the growers and sell them on commission to shops. In St Martin's Market, a new one completed in 1957, farmers and market gardeners can bring in their own goods and sell from the lorry. The old fish market was demolished when St Martin's Circus was built, and fish selling moved to Smithfield Market. The construction of a wide one-way road round the wholesale market zone has started and a new Meat, Fish and Poultry Market was opened on 18 February 1974. Later Smithfield Market will be rebuilt.

3.5 The Birmingham market zone in 1970 (based on Ordnance Survey)

3.6 Outside pulpit of St Martin's Church

3.7 Open market: Bull Ring

Inside the inner ring road

Fig. 3.8 is a simple sketch of the main land use within the inner ring road. Notice that:

1. The area of land is quite small, about half a square mile (about one square kilometre).

2. Shops and department stores, municipal buildings, offices, cathedral, railway station, cinemas and theatres cover much of the area.

3.8   Sketch of land use within inner ring road in Birmingham City Centre

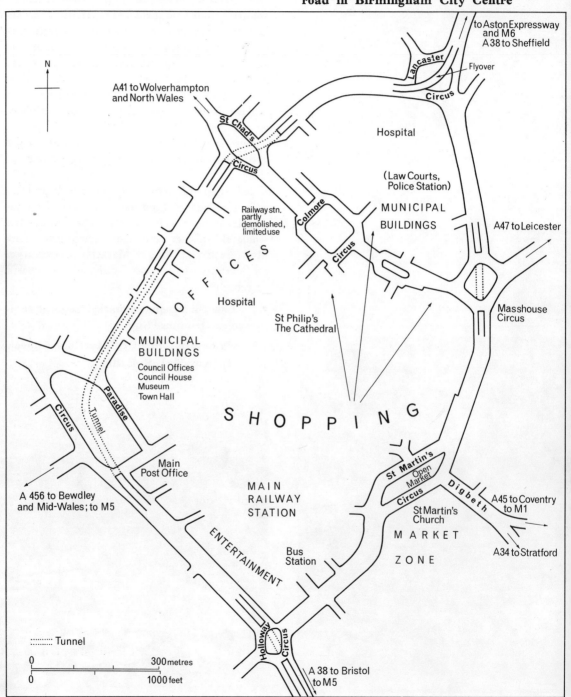

N

A41 to Wolverhampton and North Wales

St Chad's Circus

to Aston Expressway and M6
A 38 to Sheffield

Lancaster Circus

Flyover

Hospital

(Law Courts, Police Station)

Railway stn. partly demolished, limited use

Colmore Circus

MUNICIPAL BUILDINGS

A47 to Leicester

O F F I C E S

Hospital

St Philip's The Cathedral

Masshouse Circus

MUNICIPAL BUILDINGS
Council Offices
Council House
Museum
Town Hall

Paradise Circus

Tunnel

S H O P P I N G

Main Post Office

A 456 to Bewdley and Mid-Wales; to M5

St Martin's Circus

Open Market

Digbeth

A45 to Coventry to M1

MAIN RAILWAY STATION

St Martin's Church

M A R K E T

A34 to Stratford

E N T E R T A I N M E N T

Bus Station

Z O N E

.... Tunnel

0   300 metres
0   1000 feet

Holloway Circus

A 38 to Bristol to M5

16

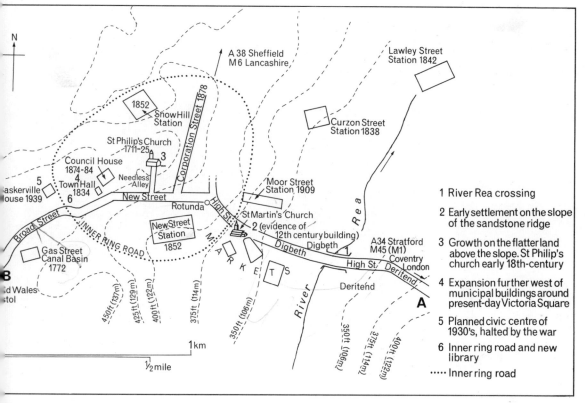

Map labels:

N

A 38 Sheffield M 6 Lancashire

Lawley Street Station 1842

1852 Snow Hill Station

Corporation Street 1878

Curzon Street Station 1838

St Philip's Church 1711-25

Council House 1874-84

Needless Alley

5 Baskerville House 1939

4 Town Hall 1834

6

New Street

Rotunda

Moor Street Station 1909

St Martin's Church 2 (evidence of 12th century building)

Broad Street

Gas Street Canal Basin 1772

INNER RING ROAD

New Street Station 1852

High St.

MARKETS

Digbeth Digbeth

A34 Stratford M45 (M1) Coventry London

High St. Deritend

River Rea

Deritend

B

d Wales stol

450ft (137m) 425ft (129m) 400ft (122m) 375ft (114m) 350ft (106m)

350ft (106m) 375ft (114m) 400ft (122m)

1 km

½ mile

A

1 River Rea crossing

2 Early settlement on the slope of the sandstone ridge

3 Growth on the flatter land above the slope. St Philip's church early 18th-century

4 Expansion further west of municipal buildings around present-day Victoria Square

5 Planned civic centre of 1930's, halted by the war

6 Inner ring road and new library

····· Inner ring road

3.9   A walk through Central Birmingham

3. Buildings with the same use tend to be near each other, for example, the large shops. An exception is the many banks scattered over the area. Large new buildings have been built for the Bank of England, Midland Bank, and National Westminster Bank since the photograph (Fig. 3.1) was taken.

This is the part of Birmingham with an increasing car parking problem.

Despite new markets, new roads, new buildings, it is still possible to pick out the old core around which Birmingham grew. The best way to learn about a town is to walk through it. We can follow a route making six stops to look at evidence of the different periods which have been significant in the development of the city. The map (Fig. 3.9), showing the roads to be followed from A to B and the six stopping places, also gives an idea of the height of the land by including contour lines.

Starting at the crossing of the River Rea (1), walk uphill following the medieval route to St Martin's Church, the Bull Ring and the markets (2). Pass under the ring road and use the modern outside escalator to reach the Rotunda and go along New Street. Diverge up Needless Alley, a narrow road leading to the cathedral, St Philip's Church (3). Return to New Street and continue to the Town Hall and Council House (4) in the area of nineteenth-century expansion. Near here a new civic centre was planned just before the outbreak of the Second World War. Baskerville House (5) was one municipal office building which was completed. The foundation stone will tell you when it was built. The final stop (6) is at an example of the rebuilding of Birmingham along the inner ring road. The new library complex near the Town Hall, which the planners say is the biggest in Europe, has replaced the Victorian Reference Library.

The gradual development of the City Centre westwards is brought out in the profile of the walk (Fig. 3.10). It also provides a summary of the important points made about Birmingham in this chapter.

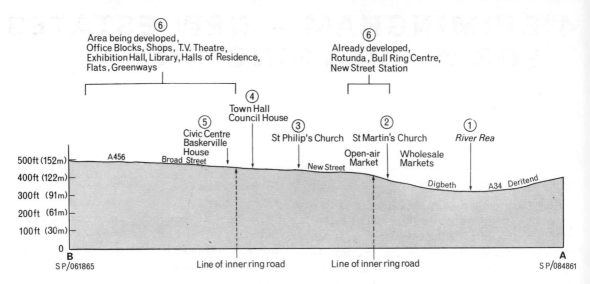

3.10 Profile of walk from Deritend to Broad Street, as shown on Fig. 3.9

Exercises. 1. (a) Draw a simple sketch-map to show the position of Birmingham's markets alongside St Martin's Church and the inner ring road in 1970. Make sure that you label the different markets.

    (b) Find out what changes have taken place in the wholesale market zone since 1970.

2. Birmingham's markets are placed in and around the Bull Ring. Why is this?

3. What is the difference between a retail and a wholesale market?

4. In the open market (Fig. 3.7), there is often a great deal of litter lying about. Clearing this is just one of the problems of running a market. What others would there be?

5. Draw a sketch-map to show where the markets are in your own town. Check if your local library has copies of old maps showing the market sites. Write down all the facts you can about your markets. Put your work under headings, such as Kinds of Markets, Problems of the Markets, Sources of the Produce, Areas Served by the Markets.

6. Use an encyclopaedia or reference book and explain what is meant by each of the following: Domesday Book, a market charter, a toll, a cold store, an abattoir.

7. Choose a road leading across the centre of your town. Using an Ordnance Survey map, scale 6 inches to a mile, (a) trace the road and the contour lines, (b) draw a profile as in Fig. 3.10. Walk along the road looking for foundation stones on the largest buildings and dates on houses. You can mark these on your map in a similar way to Fig. 3.9. Churches, houses, schools, factories and railway stations are built for people to use. They are a sign of growth of a town. Choose some of the buildings marked on your map and find out why they were built. What do they tell about the history of your town?

8. The Rotunda office block is shown on Figs. 3.1 and 3.2. What other types of buildings can be identified?

9. A city has several functions. For instance, it may be a market centre, an administrative centre, a shopping centre, an entertainment centre. List the functions of Birmingham City Centre.

4 | BIRMINGHAM – NEW ESTATES FOR A CHANGING CITY

I. INSIDE THE CITY

Birmingham grew as a market town at a convenient crossing place of the little River Rea; but it also developed as an industrial centre. It was midway between two contrasting regions. To the north and west in Staffordshire was an area rich in iron ore and coal, whereas to the south and east in Warwickshire lay good farming land. Metal brought from Staffordshire was fashioned into knives, nails and farming implements by smiths living along High Street near the river.

No doubt these goods were sold or exchanged for food or meat.

By the mid-nineteenth century Birmingham's industries of brass articles, jewellery, guns, and iron and steel goods had grown rapidly. Alongside the small factories hundreds of houses for the workers were built. There were no trams, buses or cars. The factories, houses, schools, shops and churches had to be within walking distance of each other. The houses were small, dark, without water or sanitation and built either back-to-back

4.1 Ordnance Survey map of two Birmingham streets (1888)

4.2 Ordnance Survey map of Birmingham streets (1905)

or round a courtyard. An Ordnance Survey map for 1888 (Fig. 4.1) shows part of Pigott Street and Bath Row, typical Birmingham streets of this time. In Pigott Street four houses facing the street were backed by four more facing two courtyards. In these courtyards there were eight houses, the water tap (W.T.) for the sixteen houses, two wash houses and privies (toilets). An improvement on these were the tunnel-back houses. They were long and narrow, each with its own scullery and W.C. (toilet). There was a garden at the back and often at the front, as in Bath Row.

These houses along Pigott Street are shown also in the 1905 map (Fig. 4.2). Look at their shape, remember which is the back-to-back, the courtyard and the tunnel-back. Find similar houses in other parts of the map. The latter shows a jumble of houses, factories, schools and churches in the Bath Row area about half a mile (about one kilometre) from the City Centre. The map was typical of many of the streets near the centre of Birmingham until quite recently.

Before the bombing in the Second World War, there were still 38,000 back-to-back houses and over 100,000 tunnel-backs in Birmingham. In the older quarters of the city, the houses and buildings were shabby. People wanted better sanitation and electricity. Schools were old, with little or no play space, and there were few parks. The factories and workshops added to the noise, smoke and dirt. The narrow streets were used by vans, lorries, cars, trams and buses.

These poor conditions occurred not only in Birmingham, but in other large cities where industry had developed in the nineteenth century. The factories and houses, often of a poor standard, were built too quickly and too close together. Today, we call such a derelict area in a city a 'twilight zone'.

In 1946 Birmingham City Council decided to improve the large twilight zone in the city. It bought 1,000 acres (405 hectares) of land in five districts, now named Lee Bank, Ladywood, Newtown, Nechells Green and Highgate (Fig. 4.3).

The chief aims were to:
1. rebuild the houses, shopping centres and schools,
2. design a new road pattern,
3. provide open spaces,

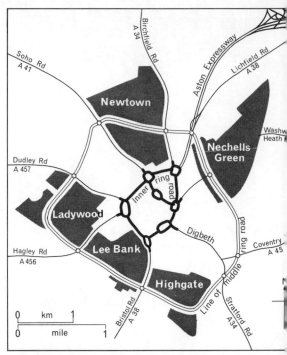

4.3 Birmingham Comprehensive Development Areas (C.D.A.s)

4. separate different land uses such as industry, housing, offices and shops.

Each of the five new districts was to be developed as a separate community to be linked by roads and open spaces. A district was called a Comprehensive Development Area, or C.D.A. for short.

The crowded Bath Row area was one of the districts to be rebuilt. It was even given a new name, Lee Bank. The photograph, Fig. 4.4, was taken during rebuilding. Some roads are named on the sketch, Fig. 4.5. How is Lee Bank different from the old Bath Row area it replaced? Look for changes by taking an imaginary walk up Pigott Street and along Bath Row. There are new maisonettes, a tall block of flats, running track and sports ground. Further along Holloway Head new factories have been built. Gone are the back-to-back and tunnel-back houses, the courtyards, old schools and factories.

The lay-out on the photograph suggests light and space. Grass separates the buildings. The homes are different shapes and sizes. Wide new roads are connected by footpaths. On the plan of Lee Bank (Fig. 4.6), the part shown in the aerial

4.4 Lee Bank Comprehensive Development Area (C.D.A.)

4.5 Key to Fig. 4.4

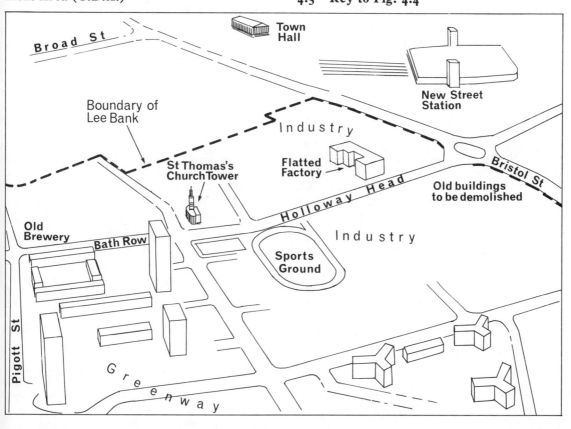

photograph is enclosed by the broken line. The complete Lee Bank district is bounded by Broad Street, Bristol Street and Lee Bank Road, with a later extension to the south. Notice that the industries, offices and main shopping areas are in separate blocks. The schools, open spaces and shopping precincts are conveniently near the homes. Because land has been used to provide areas of grass and sports grounds, there is less space for buildings. Only 6,531 people live here now, compared with 14,797 before development. At the same time, the amount of land for industry remains much the same. On the north side of Holloway Head are small and medium-sized factories mainly engaged in metal manufactures. To help very small firms to remain in the area, a seven-storey Flatted Factory has been built in Holloway Head (Fig. 4.5).

Nechells Green, Newtown, Ladywood and Highgate, the other four areas which have been redeveloped, are bigger than Lee Bank, but the lay-out and buildings are similar. Table 4.1 sets out the area of land developed, the number of dwellings, number of schools and so on. Notice how the amount of open space has been increased; for example, in Ladywood there are now 49.8 acres (19.9 hectares) compared with 1.9 acres (0.7 hectares) before redevelopment. The numbers of homes and people have dropped considerably. 102,896 people formerly lived in the five

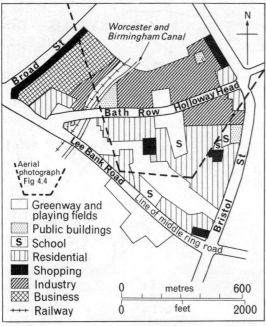

4.6 Land use in Lee Bank C.D.A.

Table 4.1 *Land use in the five Comprehensive Development Areas*

Area	Total redevelopment area	Population A (B)	No. of dwellings A (B)	No. of schools A (B)	Education Area A (B) Acres Ha	Industry A (B) Acres Ha	Public open space A (B) Acres H
Nechells Green	267.0 acres 106.8 ha	12,537 (19,072)	3,635 (5,885)	10 (12)	27.0 10.8 (8.0) (3.2)	62.4 24.9 (63.3) (25.3)	41.7 16.6 (3.9) (1.5)
Newtown	398.5 acres 159.4 ha	15,400 (28,125)	4,467 (9,349)	14 (15)	39.9 15.9 (12.9) (5.1)	118.7 47.4 (118.5) (47.4)	60.4 24.1 (6.4) (2.5)
Ladywood	289.0 acres 115.6 ha	12,448 (24,418)	3,609 (7,558)	9 (9)	25.3 10.1 (4.6) (1.8)	62.1 24.8 (61.6) (24.6)	49.8 19.9 (1.9) (0.7)
Lee Bank	192.0 acres 76.8 ha	6,531 (14,797)	1,894 (4,492)	5 (7)	12.7 5.0 (3.4) (1.3)	39.7 15.8 (44.2) (17.6)	24.7 9.8 (0.2) (0.08)
Highgate	236.0 acres 94.4 ha	10,080 (16,484)	2,924 (4,886)	15 (8)	32.1 12.8 (6.0) (2.4)	50.3 20.1 (53.4) (21.3)	39.0 15.6 (9.7) (3.8)
	1,382.5 acres 553.0 ha	56,996 (102,896)	16,529 (32,170)	53 (51)	137.0 54.8 (34.9) (13.9)	333.2 133.2 (341.0) (136.4)	215.6 86 (22.3) (8.

A After redevelopment
(B) Before redevelopment

4.7 Aerial view of Primrose Hill estate

redevelopment areas but, after the buildings had been demolished and new flats built, only 56,996 returned to live there. Where have the remaining 45,900 people found homes?

There are four ways in which the Birmingham Corporation has been tackling this problem. First, by building on such land as was available inside the city boundary. This included a disused aerodrome, a racecourse, an area of prefabricated houses built at the end of the Second World War, and some farmland. On these, five new estates are being built:

Castle Vale (aerodrome): 5,000 new homes for 21,000 people.
Bromford Bridge (racecourse): 1,900 new homes for 7,000 people.
Druid's Heath (prefabricated estate): 2,000 new homes for 8,000 people.

Primrose Hill (farmland): 812 new homes for 3,000 people.
Woodgate Valley (farmland): 4,500 new homes for 17,500 people.

Perhaps you live on one of the new estates. If so, is your home a flat, a maisonette, a bungalow, a semi-detached house, a terrace house, a split-level house or another kind? Can you walk to school, shops and the doctor's surgery along footpaths without crossing a main road? Does your estate look anything like the one at Primrose Hill in the foreground of Fig. 4.7?

This was the first large, new residential neighbourhood to be built inside the city close to the boundary. It lies near the old village centre of King's Norton, which had been swallowed up by the growth of Birmingham early in the present century. The village is marked A on Fig. 4.8.

23

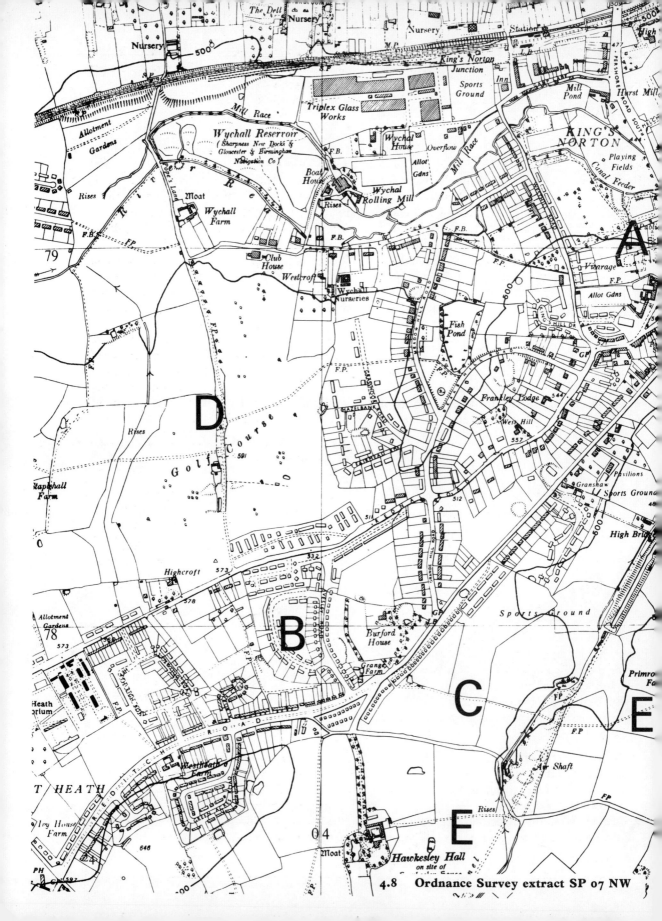

4.8 Ordnance Survey extract SP 07 NW

Beyond the village, two main roads (Rednal Road and Redditch Road), leading south-west, follow the high land, B. When this map was printed in 1952, apart from the semi-detached houses bordering these two roads, the land was used for farming and a golf course. By 1971 the land use had greatly changed. Primrose Hill Estate (C) had been built; the City had bought the golf course (D) for another housing estate, and the Secretary of State for the Environment had given permission for houses to be built on Primrose Hill Farm and farmland belonging to Hawkesley Hall (E).

One important difference between Lee Bank Estate near the City Centre and Primrose Hill on the city boundary, is that there are no local factories providing jobs at Primrose Hill. Nor are any planned for the area.

II. OUTSIDE THE CITY

Birmingham had to find homes not only for people moved from the newly developed areas inside the city, but also for the natural growth of the population as well as immigrants attracted by jobs in industry. The new estates inside the city were not enough and so building outside the city had to take place,

1. in the *Green Belt*,
2. in *Expanding Towns*,
3. in *New Towns*.

The Green Belt

By building continuously outwards from a town, the countryside disappears until finally towns join each other. This has happened already in Birmingham and the Black Country. To halt this process, the counties of Worcestershire, Warwickshire, Staffordshire and Shropshire have agreed upon a Green Belt around the cities and towns. This is shown in Fig. 4.9. It is land used mainly for agriculture and recreation. Building is allowed only for Green Belt purposes, for example farmhouses, farm buildings and sports changing rooms. The Department of the Environment will, however, consider requests to build in the Green Belt and in the case of Birmingham agreed that a slice of this land should become the new suburb of Chelmsley Wood for 60,000 people.

4.9   The Green Belt and planned growth of Birmingham

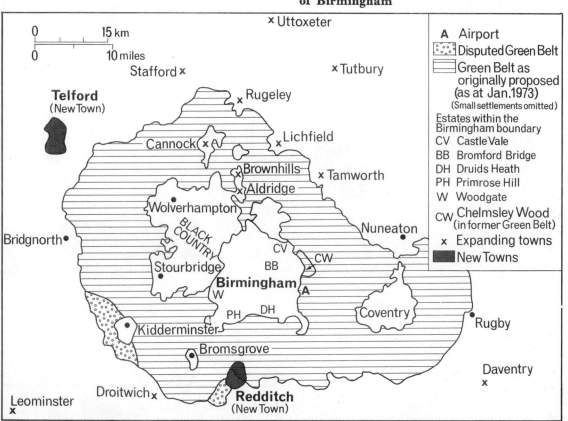

As in Lee Bank (a C.D.A.) and Primrose Hill (a boundary estate), Chelmsley Wood (in the Green Belt) has its own schools, churches, shopping centres and community halls but many more of each because it is bigger. The suburb is close to the airport and therefore two-storey houses instead of high-rise flats have been built. Each is centrally heated with a small garden, and parking space for one car per family is planned. The high rents, long distances to travel to work in Birmingham and infrequency of buses are problems for the people who have moved there. Women used to have local jobs when they lived in the older parts of Birmingham. Some light industry on this estate, which will employ mainly female labour, will help families pay the higher rents.

Expanding towns

In 1952, the 'Town Development Act' made it possible for small towns near a large city to receive population and industry from that city.

Eleven towns near Birmingham agreed schemes for building new factories and houses. They were Aldridge–Brownhills, Cannock, Daventry, Droitwich, Leominster, Lichfield, Rugeley, Stafford, Tamworth, Tutbury and Uttoxeter (Fig. 4.9). In some cases the scheme is very small and requires only the building of a few houses. At Droitwich, Tamworth and Daventry, on the other hand, the expansion will be considerable. Let us look at one of these.

The small town of Droitwich, with a population of 8,000, lies along the A38, 10 miles (16 km) south of the Birmingham boundary, and stands on the slopes of the valley of the River Salwarpe. The Romans called it Salinae, meaning the place of salt. The rocks below contain brine from which salt can be evaporated. There are salt factories nearby but none left in Droitwich itself. Where the factories once stood are now open spaces. A master plan for developing Droitwich was drawn up (Fig. 4.10), by the Droitwich Deve-

4.10 Master plan for Droitwich

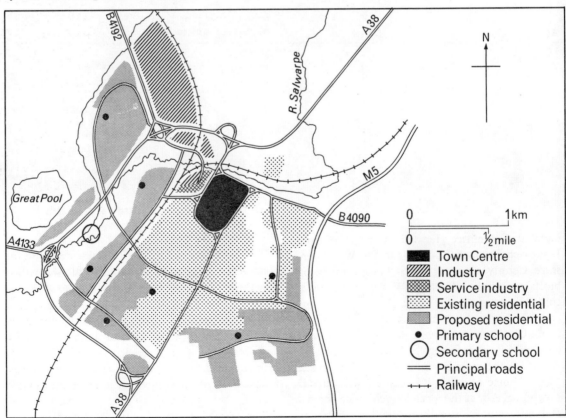

0 — 1km
0 — ½ mile

- ■ Town Centre
- ▨ Industry
- ▤ Service industry
- ⬚ Existing residential
- ▦ Proposed residential
- ● Primary school
- ○ Secondary school
- ═ Principal roads
- ┼┼┼ Railway

4.11   The Square, Sutton Hill, Telford

lopment Committee, formed of members from Droitwich Borough Council and the Worcestershire County Council: 6,000 houses are being built beyond the old town, and Birmingham is contributing money for 2,000 of these for tenants and key workers moving out with Birmingham firms. On the industrial site, a firm can lease land and build its own factory or lease a factory unit. By 1981 the population is expected to reach 30,000. Some of you will live in a town which is expanding. Ask at the local council office about a plan and compare it with the one for Droitwich.

The New Towns

The New Towns Act, 1946, tried to deal with the desperate housing shortage of the post-war period without adding to the outward sprawl of the big cities. The Government choose sites for New Towns beyond the Green Belt and appoint Development Corporations to build new houses, shops, offices and factories needed in them. Stevenage in Hertfordshire was the first of these New Towns. Like most of the early ones, it served the London area where the housing need was most urgent. The first New Town for the West Midlands was

27

Dawley, now renamed Telford. It was not designated until 1963 and was followed by Redditch in 1964.

Telford New Town

The people in the square in Fig. 4.11 probably lived originally in Birmingham, in one of the older parts of the town. They now have modern houses, such as those in the background, in Sutton Hill which forms part of the New Town of Telford. Telford is near the Welsh border, in Shropshire, 22 miles (35 km) west of the Birmingham boundary. Over the next twenty years, 100,000 people will find homes here and the population is expected to grow from 69,000 in 1966 to 225,000 by 1991.

Much of the site is a plateau area between 400 and 700 feet (122–215 m) above sea level, cut through in the south by the gorge of the River Severn. To the north the land drops sharply to the smaller River Tern. The hilly mass of the Wrekin and Ercall rising to over 1,300 feet (400 m) shelters the town on the west.

Coalbrookdale (Fig. 4.12) is often described as the birthplace of the Industrial Revolution. Here in 1709 Abraham Darby began smelting iron ore, using coke instead of charcoal for fuel. Local coal, ironstone, limestone and water power were available. The River Severn, later supplemented by canals, provided transport. A thriving iron and steel industry produced the first cast-iron bridge in the world in 1777, over the River Severn at Ironbridge. Thomas Telford, who lived from 1757 to 1834, was at one time Surveyor of Public Works for Shropshire. He became the most famous road-bridge and aqueduct builder of his age. He used iron to build factories also. His name was chosen for the New Town.

Alongside Coalbrookdale, the small settlements of Dawley, Madeley and Coalport developed, the latter being famous for coalport china in its day. To the north the larger towns of Oakengates and Wellington still have important iron and steel industries. There are iron foundries, firms producing cast-iron goods, structural steel work, engineering tools, fire-clay products, as well as clay quarries and open-cast mining.

The New Town planners were faced with:
1. an existing population of 69,000 in several small towns and villages;
2. much uneven land resulting from quarrying and shallow mining;
3. few naturally flat areas for large-scale industrial development.

To make one town from all these elements is no quick easy task. Factories, houses, schools, shops, roads and services must be developed simultaneously. A new area has to be built around the old.

In order to do this, it was decided to group a total of 8,000 homes, old and new, into one community. Sutton Hill (Fig. 4.11) is an example. The photograph shows the community centre for the 8,000 homes. Here is the Child Welfare Clinic, doctor's and dentist's surgeries, meeting rooms, coffee bar and lounge, library, pastoral centre, public house and shops. Each community has a primary school.

Three such communities form one district for which there is a comprehensive secondary school and shopping centre. In each district established factories have room to expand. New industrial sites will provide space for Birmingham firms to move out to Telford.

The first district to be developed is in the south. It is called *Madeley* and includes the existing settlements of Coalbrookdale, Ironbridge, Madeley and Coalport (Fig. 4.12). Sutton Hill (S.H.) was the first housing area completed in this district. Quite near are the industrial sites of Halesfield (H) and Tweedale (T), already occupied by over fifty firms. The famous Ironbridge Gorge is in Madeley District, and will be cleared for parkland. 'The Ironbridge Gorge Museum Trust Ltd' has set up an open-air museum where examples of old techniques in iron-making, tramway and canal transport are being reconstructed.

On Fig. 4.13, the different districts which will eventually make up Telford are named. The second district, *Stirchley*, is already under way, with its industrial estate at Stafford Park (SP).

Communications from one district to another and from Telford to Birmingham are most important. The main roads and railways serving the built-up areas before the building of Telford are

28

4.12 Telford New Town

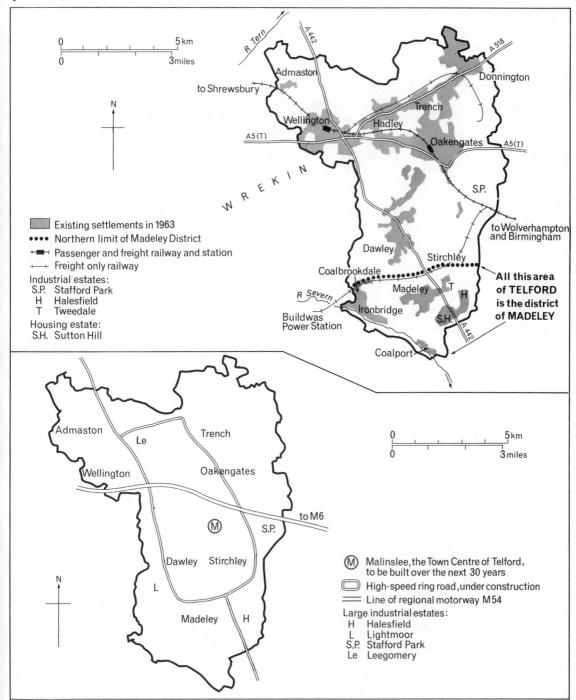

Existing settlements in 1963
Northern limit of Madeley District
Passenger and freight railway and station
Freight only railway

Industrial estates:
S.P. Stafford Park
H   Halesfield
T   Tweedale

Housing estate:
S.H. Sutton Hill

All this area of TELFORD is the district of MADELEY

M Malinslee, the Town Centre of Telford, to be built over the next 30 years
High-speed ring road, under construction
Line of regional motorway M54

Large industrial estates:
H   Halesfield
L   Lightmoor
S.P. Stafford Park
Le   Leegomery

4.13 The districts of Telford New Town

shown on Fig. 4.12. In the next ten years the districts will be linked by a high-speed ring road (Fig. 4.13). Most important is the decision to build the M54 as a motorway link between Telford and Birmingham. In time perhaps the railway will be electrified and an additional station built for the new Town Centre, to be called Malinslee.

To make Telford a success there must be jobs for people who move there. The New Town Corporation is providing four major industrial sites (Fig. 4.13) and many smaller ones. The problems are to attract manufacturing firms to factories in Telford, and to persuade skilled factory workers to leave Birmingham and the Black Country and live in Telford.

New buildings, new roads, new parks must fit like a jigsaw puzzle into the villages and towns already there. The result will be Telford in A.D. 2000.

Redditch New Town

Five miles south of the Birmingham boundary is the town of Redditch, the chief centre in the country for needlemaking. This is a very old craft, at one time dependent on water power provided by mills on the River Arrow. To the west of the river is a ridge of upland on which a Victorian town, with small factories producing needles and fishing tackle, grew steadily. By 1964 the population was 29,000, of which 13,000 were employed in manufacturing industry, including engineering and metal goods. Factories were small, employing much female labour and out-workers. An outworker works at home. Putting needles into a packet is the kind of job done by an outworker.

Redditch New Town was designated in 1964 to take 'overspill' population from Birmingham. The boundary included parts of Redditch Urban

4.14 Redditch New Town

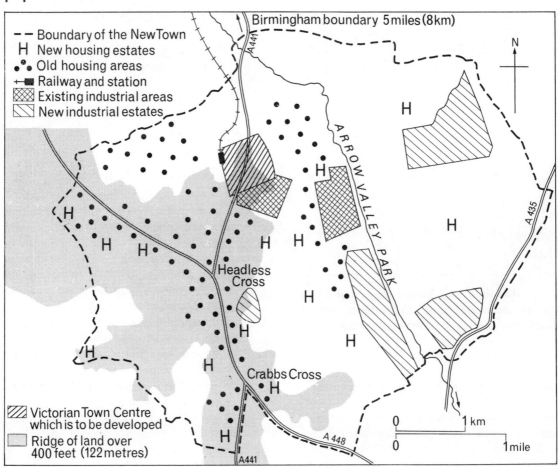

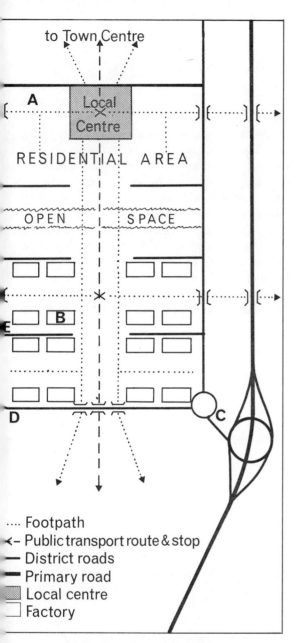

4.15 Redditch New Town: suggested layout for an industrial area and adjoining residential area with footpaths and roads

District, and took in more of the Arrow Valley, including its eastern slopes (Fig. 4.14). New housing estates with adjoining industrial centres were to spread across the valley and its slopes, with a park following the river. Fig. 4.15 is a diagram of the layout of an industrial estate

separated by an open space from a housing area. If you lived at house A, you could walk along a footpath to work at factory B. On a wet day, you might catch a bus at the local centre and ride through the middle of the estate to the stop near the factory. On the other hand, van drivers delivering goods would drive from the main road link at C, along the encircling district road D to the access road at E. The houses, factories, paths and roads have been planned so that pedestrians and vehicles are separated.

At certain times in the history of Britain a tremendous burst of town building has taken place. We are living in such a period. Birmingham, Droitwich, Telford and Redditch are examples, but there are many more.

Look at the Town Centre Plan for Redditch in the year 1991 (Fig. 4.16). The plan was published in 1968 and bit by bit, over the next twenty years, this will take shape. It is likely that some details of the plan will change, but notice:

1. The large traffic-free area.
2. There is only one through 'bus route'.
3. Traffic moves round a ring road with access to the centre.
4. The housing is mainly outside the ring road.
5. The shops, civic, business, cultural and entertainment buildings occupy the town centre.
6. The parish church is the central building.

These six ideas are repeated in other Town Centres which are developing. The Redditch Town Centre will serve an estimated population of between 70,000 and 80,000 by 1991.

All the new building we have been reading about in these two chapters will give some Birmingham people much better homes and an improved environment, but there are problems such as the following:

1. Multi-storey flats are not popular.
2. Rents of new flats and houses are high.
3. Some new estates have no local jobs for women.
4. A New Town needs to attract industry before people will move there.
5. People of all age groups, not simply young married couples, are needed in a New Town.

Can you suggest how these can be solved?

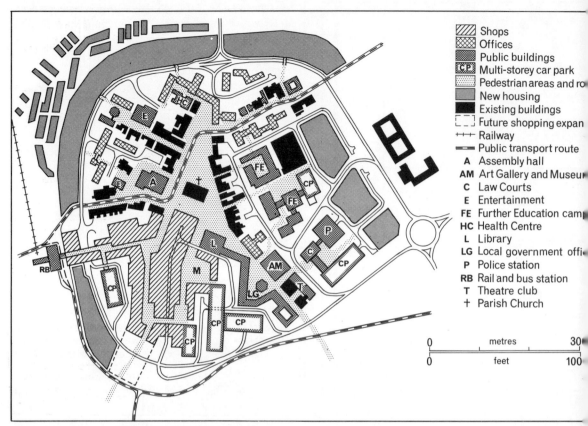

Legend:

- Shops
- Offices
- Public buildings
- CP Multi-storey car park
- Pedestrian areas and ro[...]
- New housing
- Existing buildings
- Future shopping expan[...]
- +++ Railway
- === Public transport route
- A Assembly hall
- AM Art Gallery and Museu[...]
- C Law Courts
- E Entertainment
- FE Further Education cam[...]
- HC Health Centre
- L Library
- LG Local government offi[...]
- P Police station
- RB Rail and bus station
- T Theatre club
- + Parish Church

Scale:
0 metres 30[...]
0 feet 100[...]

4.16 Redditch New Town: Town Centre plan for 1991

Exercises Use Fig. 4.2 to answer the following questions:

1. (a) Put a piece of tracing paper over the map and copy the roads. Name these.
   (b) For each of the following, draw the outline and print the name:
      St Thomas's Church, Schools, Chapel.
   (c) Copy a block of back-to-back houses and a block of tunnel-back houses.
   (d) The larger shaded blocks are factories; show two or three examples by shading and overprinting with the letter F.
   (e) By St Thomas's Church there is this mark ↑ B.M. 472.4. This is called a Bench Mark. The arrow represents the one cut into the brick or stone of a building. The number is the height in feet above sea level. Add it onto your tracing paper and any other similar arrows and numbers. Ring round the highest and lowest numbers.
   (f) The school on the map was the largest church school in Birmingham in 1903, with 1220 pupils. Allowing two children to each house, estimate how many lived in the roads around the school. Is this many or few?
   (g) From Fig. 4.2 print on your tracing any name which suggests that this was once a rural area.
2. From the evidence on the map, Fig. 4.2, write a short description of this area as it was in 1905.
3. The aerial photograph of Lee Bank (Fig. 4.4) was taken in 1969. Identify the tower

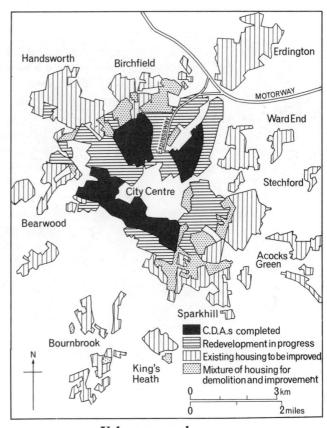

4.17 **Urban renewal**

of St Thomas's Church (the rest was destroyed in the last war). Although some of the road pattern is new, Pigott Street, Bath Row and Cregoe Street remain, and you can work out roughly the part which would cover the map, Fig. 4.2. Compare the photograph and the map. What has replaced the school? What other changes have taken place?

4. In Question 2 you described the area using the 1905 map. Now describe the area as it was in 1969, using the photograph, Fig. 4.4.

5. What is a 'flatted factory'? The one in Holloway Head was the first in Birmingham. Where else in the city is there one?

6. (a) Draw a rectangle the same size as Fig. 4.8.
    (b) Add and number the grid lines and give a key to symbols.
    (c) Add the railway line, Rednal Road, Redditch Road, the canal and its tunnel passing between Hawkesley Hall and Primrose Hill Farm.
    (d) Draw in the River Rea and the 500-ft (152-m) contour line.
    (e) Within this valley name five different uses of the land.
    (f) Print 'golf course' and 'farmland' in the correct places.

7. What is meant by a Green Belt? Find out about London's Green Belt.

8. Modern estates in Birmingham, the New Towns and expanding towns in the West Midlands are being planned very carefully. The examples in Chapters 2 and 3 explain some of the more important features of the estates. For instance, primary schools are

33

so placed that pupils can reach the school along footpaths and do not need to cross roads. What were the aims in planning (a) the dwellings, (b) transport, (c) shops, (d) industry?

9. Select a New Town from outside the West Midlands and obtain information on:
   (a) Why the site was chosen for a New Town.
   (b) The general layout of the town.
   (c) The detail of housing and industrial estates.
   (d) Communications.

10. Birmingham had so many derelict houses and buildings near the city centre that the policy was to clear whole districts and rebuild. On Fig. 4.17 these are shown in the key as the C.D.A.s and the areas where development is in progress. The plan for the future is different. There are pockets of solid but rather drab pre-1914 houses. These will not be demolished. The neighbourhood is to be tidied up and property owners can improve their houses with the aid of a grant.
    (a) What is meant in the map key by 'mixture of housing' for demolition and improvement'?
    (b) Urban renewal is the continual rebuilding and improvement of a town. Describe the areas of renewal which are passed through on a journey from the city centre to King's Heath.
    (c) In the years between the wars, that is 1918 to 1939, many Council and private housing estates were built in Birmingham. Kingstanding is an example which can be located on Ordnance Survey Map B.2. Find out the names of similar districts.

5 | COMMUNICATIONS

1. Canals

Goods and people move from place to place by water, rail, road and air. A hundred and fifty years ago canals formed a network over much of the country. Few railways had yet been built and roads were poor. From Birmingham it was possible to send goods along canals and navigable rivers to the Mersey, Humber, Severn and Thames estuaries and so to the ports of Liverpool, Hull, Gloucester and London.

Locally the Birmingham Canal was the most important. Along this small waterway coal, iron, limestone, clay and bricks moved from the South Staffordshire coalfield to the growing foundries and factories of Birmingham and the Black Country. The original winding canal built by James Brindley in 1769 was straightened by Thomas Telford in 1824. The loops which were left, plus other branching arms and basins, provided miles of wharfage for factories.

To find out where the canals of the Midlands meet, go to Gas Street in the centre of Birmingham. Pass through an archway in the wall and descend some steps into the canal basin shown on the aerial photograph (Fig. 5.1) and named on the sketch (Fig. 5.2). Suddenly you are away from the noise of the big city. Signs of the past use of the canals are all around (Fig. 5.3). Here the Birmingham Canal meets the Worcester and Birmingham Canal. Originally a bar 84 yards (76.8 m) long and about 7 feet (2 m) wide divided the Birmingham Basin from the Worcester Basin. It was called the Worcester Bar. Goods had to be lifted over it from one canal to the other and there was a toll house for each canal. Later the bar was cut by a level lock to allow boats through. This small, quiet canal basin was once a noisy, lively thoroughfare at the centre of the canal system of England. From Worcester Bar, narrow-boats could set out through the canals named on Fig. 5.4 to reach the estuaries.

Canal construction was not easy. Remember that Birmingham lies on a plateau some 400 feet (122 m) above sea level, fringed by the valleys of the Rivers Trent, Severn and Avon. Descent to these valleys had to be made by locks, which wasted water, limited the size of boats and the tonnage carried, and slowed down the journey. On the plateau itself more locks were used where there was a change of slope and tunnels were pierced through the Ridge (Fig. 2.1). To maintain the level of water needed for loaded boats was a big problem. The loss of water from evaporation and the working of the locks had to be made good from specially constructed reservoirs and from water pumped up from collieries.

Unfortunately for the canal companies, by the time this waterway system was working successfully, the cheaper, quicker railways had been built. Gradually the long-distance traffic was taken over by the railways. Local movement of coal, iron and limestone remained important, but this in turn has ceased with the working out of the South Staffordshire coalfield (Fig. 2.7).

The canals meeting in Birmingham (Fig. 5.4) are now classified as cruiseways, and there is little commercial craft on them. Factories, warehouses and high walls line the canal sides and it is difficult to find a way down to the towpath and old wharves. This was necessary for security when laden narrow-boats lay alongside. With fewer narrow-boats and obsolete warehouses, the canals have become isolated and neglected.

The recent extensive rebuilding in Central Birmingham provided an excellent opportunity for a new canalside lay-out. The City of Birmingham and British Waterways worked together to combine canal and housing in one attractive landscape. They changed the dreary industrial canal with its derelict wharves and warehouses (Fig. 5.5) into the lively centre shown in the photograph (Fig. 5.6). The Birmingham and Fazeley Canal in its later stage climbs up from the valley of the River Rea by thirteen

5.1   Aerial view of Gas Street Basin (1958)

5.2   Key to Fig. 5.1

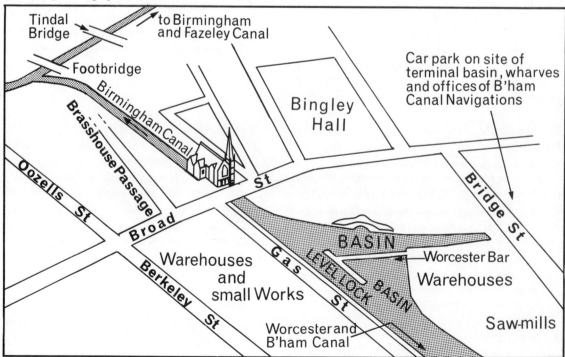

locks to meet the Birmingham Canal at Farmer's Bridge. Although the name is still used, the actual bridge disappeared more than a hundred years ago. It crossed the canal from a point just about where the man and boy are walking in Fig. 5.6. The viewpoint from which the 'before' and 'after' photographs were taken has been marked on the map of the canalside, Fig. 5.7. Overlooking the canal junction and the top four locks are tall blocks of flats. Around an old wharfside, a new public house called 'The Longboat' stands next to some restored eighteenth- and nineteenth-century cottages.

One day not long before I finished this book, I was standing looking across this canal, when from under the main bridge a horse came into sight towing a narrow-boat into the top lock. I had been lucky enough to see the only working horse on this stretch of the canal. After watching the boat move away under Tindal Bridge in the direction of the Gas Street Basin, I turned and walked to Saturday Bridge along the James Brindley Walk.

Birmingham has no large river; open water in the City Centre attracts people because it is unusual. Pleased with the success of the first project, the City has plans for other stretches of urban canal, including Gas Street Basin.

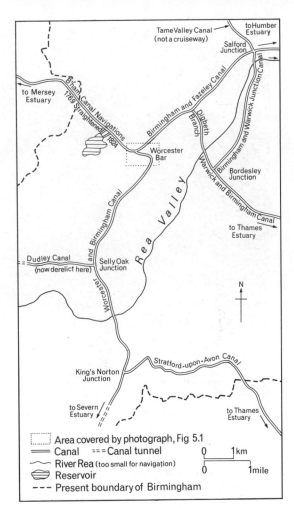

5.4 **Birmingham: the centre of the narrow canal system**

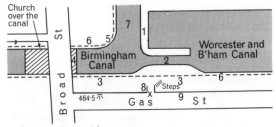

x Entrance to canal basin
1 Worcester Bar. It was 84 yd (76·8 m) long, 7 ft 3 in (2 m) wide, and goods were lifted over by crane
2 Stop lock which replaced part of the bar in 1815, allowing boats to pass through. The present gates are for flood control
3 The former toll houses
4 Evidence of three bridge structures in roof of existing canal bridge
5 Humpbacked bridge originally over the entrance to a small basin
6 Towpath for horses
7 Canal arm which led to wharves and the offices of the Birmingham Canal Navigations
8 Way down for horses, ridged bricks to prevent slipping
9 ⊕ Plaque of the Birmingham Canal Navigations

5.3 **Signs of the past in Gas Street Basin**

5.5   Top lock, Farmer's Bridge (1957)

5.6   Top lock, Farmer's Bridge (1969)

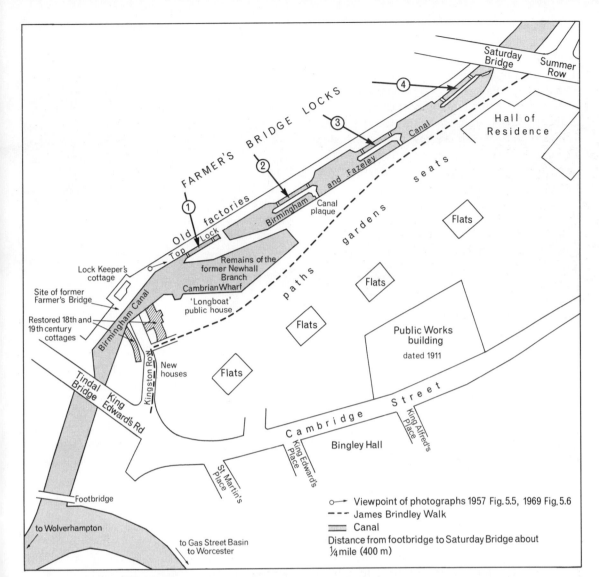

Map labels:

Saturday Bridge
Summer Row
④
Hall of Residence
③
FARMER'S BRIDGE LOCKS
and Fazeley Canal
②
Birmingham
Canal plaque
Old factories
seats
gardens
Top Lock
①
Lock Keeper's cottage
paths
Site of former Farmer's Bridge
Remains of the former Newhall Branch
Cambrian Wharf
'Longboat' public house
Restored 18th and 19th century cottages
Birmingham Canal
Flats
Flats
Flats
Flats
Public Works building
dated 1911
Tindal Bridge
King Edward's Rd
Kingston Row
New houses
Flats
St Martin's Place
King Edward's Place
King Edward's Place
Cambridge Street
King Alfred's Place
Bingley Hall
Footbridge
to Wolverhampton
to Gas Street Basin
to Worcester

o—o Viewpoint of photographs 1957 Fig. 5.5, 1969 Fig. 5.6
- - - James Brindley Walk
▦ Canal
Distance from footbridge to Saturday Bridge about ¼ mile (400 m)

5.7   Canalside development in Birmingham: James Brindley Walk

Sixty-six miles (106 km) of canal, part of the Birmingham Canal Navigations in Birmingham and the Black Country, were in danger of being drained and filled in. It has now been suggested that the canals could be maintained if local authorities will pay towards restoration and upkeep. It may be cheaper to maintain a canal than fill it in. Even though a canal is no longer used for trade, it may still have a number of uses, such as supplying water to industry, providing a drainage channel for surplus water, and recreational pursuits, e.g. canoeing and fishing.

5.8   Bronze plaque, James Brindley Walk

JAMES BRINDLEY WALK

THIS PLAQUE COMMEMORATES THE OPENING OF JAMES BRINDLEY WALK AND WAS UNVEILED BY THE LORD MAYOR ALD. N.B.A. BOSWORTH J.L.B. ON SATURDAY 26TH JULY 1969

THE CANAL SIDE WALK STANDS ON THE SITE OF THE NEWHALL BRANCH PART OF THE ORIGINAL BIRMINGHAM CANAL BUILT BY JAMES BRINDLEY IN 1769

THIS CANAL LAID THE FOUNDATION OF THE BIRMINGHAM CANAL NAVIGATIONS AND CONTRIBUTED SIGNIFICANTLY TO THE COMMERCIAL PROSPERITY OF THE CITY OF BIRMINGHAM.

1769   1969

Alongside the canal (Fig. 5.7) is the James Brindley Walk, commemorated by a plaque reproduced as Fig. 5.8. The wording on the plaque recalls that Birmingham's canal, in an area without navigable rivers, played an important part in the development of industry by enabling heavy material to be transported. James Brindley Walk also shows how canals, although no longer of commercial importance, can make a contribution to recreation and landscapes in a town.

2. Railways

If the canals in the Birmingham area are no longer used commercially, what about the railways? In 1837 the first railway line from Liverpool reached Birmingham. The next year the line to London was opened. In less than twenty years the main railway network around Birmingham was built (Fig. 5.9). Manufacturers wanted goods to be carried more quickly than by canal. At first the trains were used for goods and for passengers travelling long distances; there were few stations. As factories and houses were built near the railway lines, more stations were opened. New lines joined the suburbs to the Town Centre (Fig. 5.9). This railway network still exists in 1974, except for two suburban lines which have been closed and the track removed. Extensive changes, however, have been made in the use of the lines and the stations.

Inter-City electric expresses enable Birmingham to be reached in only 95 minutes from London, Liverpool and Manchester. The two earliest lines, marked 1 and 2 in Fig. 5.9, are now combined to form the London (Euston)–Birmingham–Liverpool, electrified, trunk rail route. Steam engines have been replaced by electric locomotives (Fig. 5.10). There were formerly two main-line terminal stations, Snow Hill and New Street. Now there is one station, New Street, which has been rebuilt and enlarged.

Over the last five years there has been a remarkable change in methods of handling freight on the railways. Certain stations located at industrial centres have become freightliner terminals. High-speed container trains travel between these terminals. A firm books train space for a container. This container may belong to Freightliners Ltd, or to the firm or a road haulier.

It is loaded at the firm's premises, then taken by road transport to the train at a freightliner terminal. Transfer from road to rail takes two minutes by crane (Fig. 5.11). The flat rail wagons are permanently coupled together and form a 1,000-foot (308 m) train. On most routes the trains run overnight and delivery is completed next morning by road. Containers are of standard

5.9 Railways in the Birmingham area. Some railway stations have been added on routes to help identify modern lines. Inset shows former terminal stations.

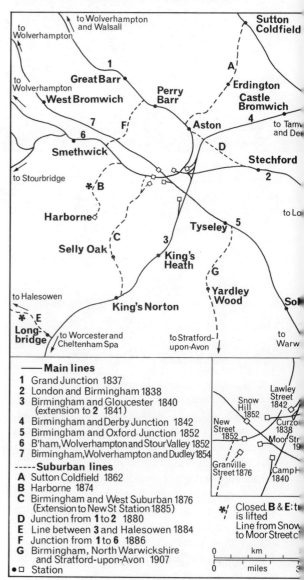

—— Main lines
1 Grand Junction 1837
2 London and Birmingham 1838
3 Birmingham and Gloucester 1840
   (extension to 2 1841)
4 Birmingham and Derby Junction 1842
5 Birmingham and Oxford Junction 1852
6 B'ham, Wolverhampton and Stour Valley 1852
7 Birmingham, Wolverhampton and Dudley 1854
----- Suburban lines
A Sutton Coldfield 1862
B Harborne 1874
C Birmingham and West Suburban 1876
   (Extension to New St Station 1885)
D Junction from 1 to 2 1880
E Line between 3 and Halesowen 1884
F Junction from 1 to 6 1886
G Birmingham, North Warwickshire
   and Stratford-upon-Avon 1907
● □ Station

5.10 **Express train between Birmingham and London**

sizes. They can be 10, 20, 30 or 40 feet long (approximately 3, 6, 9 or 12 m long). Some are covered, as in Fig. 5.11; others are open. For meat and other perishable goods, insulated ones are used.

There are two freightliner terminals in the West Midlands. The first opened at Dudley in 1967. In that year 800 containers were despatched from Dudley, but by 1969 the number had risen to 27,900. Freightliner trains were operating to Glasgow, Newcastle, Stockton, Felixstowe, Harwich, Tilbury, Southampton and Heysham. Containers were being received as well as forwarded from Dudley, and business increased so rapidly that a second terminal was opened in Landor Street, Birmingham, 1 mile (1.6 km) east of the city centre. The services to Felixstowe, Harwich, Tilbury, Southampton and Heysham now start from Birmingham, together with an additional one to London. Dudley retains the Glasgow, Newcastle and Stockton routes, with an additional one to Edinburgh. Container ships go to Ireland, Europe and North America. Before being loaded onto the ship, the containers are cleared through customs. To reduce the wait at the ports, some

5.11 **A freightliner terminal**

5.12   Birmingham Inland Port

containers are cleared at the beginning of the rail journey by means of inland customs depots set up at railway stations. The Birmingham terminal includes a customs depot; in the photograph (Fig. 5.12) the customs officer and the transport driver are checking the load in the container.

Freightliner departs		
Birmingham	15.40	Day A
Freightliner arrives		
Harwich	22.05	
Container ship leaves		
Harwich	23.55	
Container ship arrives		
Zeebrugge, Belgium	06.45	Day B
Delivery to main centres in		
Western Europe		Day C

How long does it take to reach Belgium from Birmingham?

Dudley and Birmingham terminals have room to expand, so for the time being no more are necessary in the West Midlands conurbation.

Electrification, Inter-City expresses and freightliner traffic are success stories for British Rail. It is proving harder to encourage people to make more use of local trains. An advertisement (Fig. 5.13), which appeared in January 1971, was part of a campaign to win back passengers. The West Midlands is the main car-producing centre in the country. Cars and buses, not trains, take people to work. Notice from Fig. 5.13 the number of car parks at railway stations. A kind of human freightliner service!

3. Roads

Canals and railways came to Birmingham because local manufacturers wanted to move raw

5.13   Commuter rail routes around Birmingham

Introducing Westmidrail

The new name for your local rail netwo

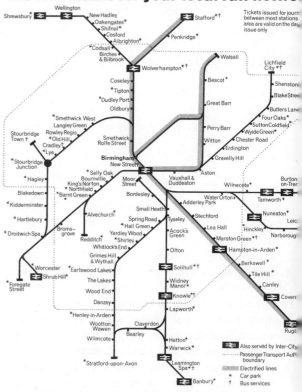

materials and goods quickly and cheaply. Canals are now disused and freightliner trains are successful because the lorry brings the container by road to the rail terminal. Motorways are the corridors along which the giant transporters, tankers, lorries, vans and cars now move. The M1 was the first motorway open and now

5.15 Ray Hall Interchange (plan)

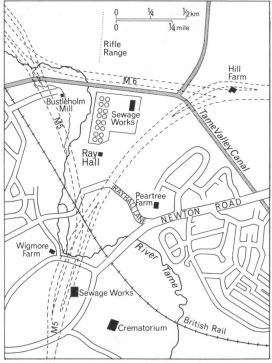

runs from London to Leeds. As more motorways were built, it was realised that a meeting place or interchange must be planned. Somewhere near the middle of England seemed sensible. The problem was to find empty land in the great sprawl of buildings which stretches for 25 miles (40 km) from Solihull to Wolverhampton. Eventually a site in West Bromwich was chosen. A photograph of the interchange in the early stages of construction, Fig. 5.14, brings out how the triangle of roads passes between housing estates and over open land. Compare this photograph with the street plan (Fig. 5.15) on which

the motorways M5 and M6 are marked by a broken line. The dark circles on the mid left of the photograph are sewage works, named on the plan. These had been built on flat, wet land near the River Tame. The latter winds its way across poor farming land which it often floods. The lowest levels of the motorways are carried on concrete stilts across the flood plain of the river. This is the Ray Hall Interchange, sometimes called the Ray Hall Triangle. There is free flow of traffic from one motorway to the other, i.e. the M5 and M6.

If we map the Midland motorways which are completed or are being built, the central position of the triangle interchange is brought out (Fig. 5.16). Notice its position in the centre of the West Midlands conurbation.

The stretch of urban motorway through the Black Country is the largest yet constructed in Britain. It runs over canals, rivers, waste tips, marlpits, old collieries, and squeezes its way between houses and factories. There are over 13 miles (21 km) of viaduct. Quite deliberately its course is through rather than round the towns, because much of the traffic on the road is for local industries.

Even more spectacular is the motorway junction at Gravelly Hill, where the M6 crosses Birmingham (Fig. 5.17). Can you wonder that it is called 'Spaghetti Junction'? This pattern of roads at different levels results from the merging of a fast new expressway with both the motorway and local roads. Birmingham is the chief city in the conurbation. Here are the television studios, the universities, the major railway station, the airport, as well as the headquarters of banks and industries. It is a regional capital. The Aston

43

Expressway has been built as a vital link from the City Centre to the M6. Sixty thousand vehicles a day are expected to use the seven-lane highway.

One of the reasons for retaining the market zone in its old central position was its access to the inner ring road, opened officially by Queen Elizabeth II in April 1971. From the markets, follow the ring road (Fig. 3.8) by way of Holloway Circus, Paradise Circus and St Chad's Circus to the fly-over at Lancaster Circus. This leads directly onto the Aston Expressway, which within two miles (3.2 km) joins the M6 at 'Spaghetti Junction'. The ring road, expressway and motor-

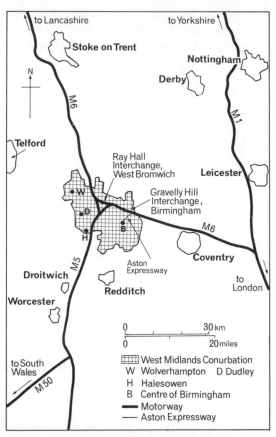

5.16 The motorway link in the West Midlands conurbation

5.17 Model of 'Spaghetti Junction', Gravelly Hill Interchange, Birmingham

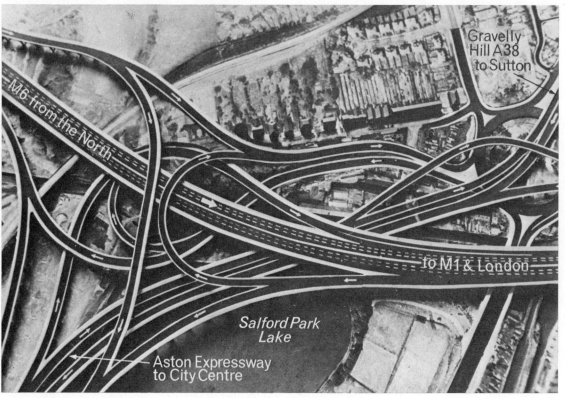

ways are purpose-built for fast traffic. Once the new market complex is built, produce will be able to flow to and fro with the minimum of hold-up. By 1972 the Midland motorways shown in Fig. 5.16 were completed and further local roads improved.

We started the chapter by thinking about Birmingham as a town 150 years ago at the centre of the silver cross of the canals. We end by seeing it once again at the centre of communications, but this time at the centre of the motorways of the 1970s.

Exercises

1. With the help of Figs. 5.1 and 5.2, draw a sketch-map of the meeting of the Birmingham Canal, Birmingham and Fazeley Canal, and the Birmingham and Worcester Canal. Name the Worcester Bar.

2. Gas Street Basin is the blue canal at grid reference 062867 on Ordnance Survey Map B.2. Starting from this point, try to follow on Map B.2 the canals you have drawn on your sketch map for Question 1. Look for reservoirs and locks. Notice the railways running close to the canals.

3. Who was James Brindley? Where did his original Birmingham canal run? How was it altered and by whom?

4. The James Brindley Walk (Fig. 5.8) won a Civic Award. What is a Civic Award and who awards it?

5. How many canalside changes can you see by comparing Figs. 5.5 and 5.6? What are the dates of these photographs?

6. What is a narrow-boat, a butty, a towpath, a hump-backed bridge, a toll house, a cruiseway?

7. A container is to be moved from Cadbury–Schweppes, Bournville, Birmingham, to Zeebrugge in Belgium, via Harwich. Use an atlas and draw a sketch map of the rail and sea route from Landor Street container terminal, Birmingham, to Zeebrugge.

8. Specialised container trains are a new way of moving bulk goods cheaply by rail. Make a collection of cuttings and illustrations, including sketches and photographs, of varied types of containers.

9. British Rail have built container ships. What is a container ship?

10. What is the difference between a container ship and a seafreight-liner, both of which sail from Harwich?

11. Why are some railway lines, which run at a loss, subsidised by Government Grants?

12. Use Fig. 5.14 and Fig. 5.15.
    (a) How many times is the River Tame crossed by the motorways in the Ray Hall Triangle?
    (b) Which buildings have had to be demolished to make way for the interchange?
    (c) Why is it called the Ray Hall Triangle?
    (d) What other means of communication does the motorway cross?
    (e) What were the main uses of the land before the motorway was built?
    (f) What buildings lie on higher ground?

13. Which road is to be built to link Telford with the M6?

14. (a) What differences are there between the Ray Hall Triangle and the Gravelly Hill Interchange ('Spaghetti Junction')?
    (b) Are there any similarities of lay-out?

15. In what ways is Birmingham a good centre of communications?

16. Locate the canal, railway line and motorway nearest to your school. For each, investigate its present use and its history.

Of the men and women employed in Birmingham, more than half are in manufacturing industry. The largest number of workers is found in the vehicle, engineering and metal trades. The pie graph, Fig. 6.1, shows that in 1969 these three trades accounted for 76 per cent of the employees in manufacturing industries. Food, chemical, rubber and printing firms were the main employers of the remaining 24 per cent.

1. Early Industries

Birmingham in the mid-nineteenth century was quite small in extent, Fig. 6.2. Its chief industries were jewellery, brass, guns and mixed metals, marked 1, Fig. 6.3. These were carried on near the City Centre in workshops and small factories sandwiched between houses.

The jewellery quarter. Look inside a ring or watch of gold or silver and you will find a group of markings. Since 1300 the law has required gold articles and, since 1544, silver ones to be marked. The testing and hallmarking are done at an Assay Office at Birmingham, London, Sheffield or Edinburgh. Each office has its own hallmark, the one for Birmingham being an anchor. Providing the mark is not too badly worn, it can tell a story. For instance the gold hallmark in Fig. 6.4 reads: 22-carat gold made in the United Kingdom by XYZ (this is the maker's registered initials) and marked in Birmingham during the year 1968-9. To help you check hallmarks, the Assay Office has published a free booklet, *British Hallmarks*.

There have been jewellers, goldsmiths and silversmiths in Birmingham for more than 200 years. The jewellery quarter is concentrated in a small area a short walk from the City Centre. Originally the master jeweller worked in his own home, but now these same houses are occupied by hundreds of small firms. Because the jeweller is a craftsman, skill is more important than machinery. Each specialises in one part of

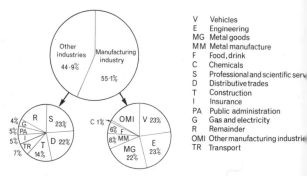

V	Vehicles
E	Engineering
MG	Metal goods
MM	Metal manufacture
F	Food, drink
C	Chemicals
S	Professional and scientific serv
D	Distributive trades
T	Construction
I	Insurance
PA	Public administration
G	Gas and electricity
R	Remainder
OMI	Other manufacturing industrie
TR	Transport

6.1 Insured employees in Birmingham (1969)

6.2 The growth of Birmingham

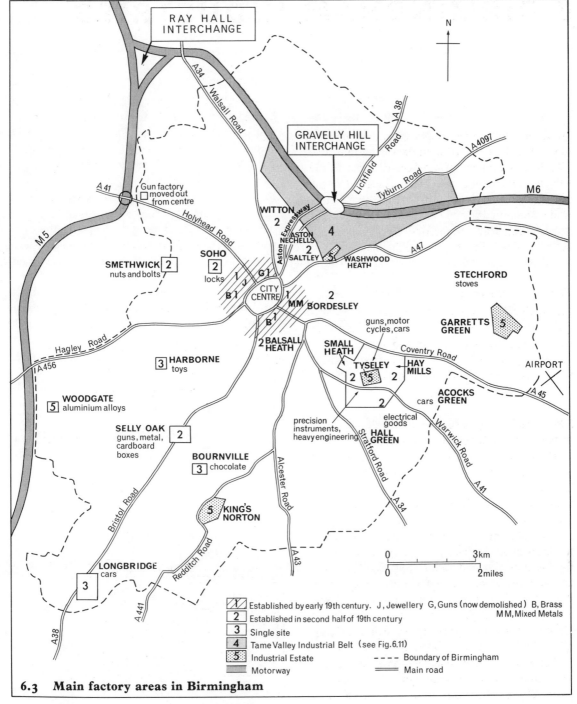

RAY HALL INTERCHANGE

GRAVELLY HILL INTERCHANGE

N

RAY HALL INTERCHANGE

Walsall Road

A34

Holyhead Road

A41

Gun factory moved out from centre

M5

Lichfield Road

A38

Tyburn Road

M6

A4097

A47

WITTON [2]

Aston Expressway

ASTON NECHELLS [2]

SALTLEY [5]

WASHWOOD HEATH

[4]

SMETHWICK [2] nuts and bolts

SOHO [2] locks

J I G1 B1

CITY CENTRE

MM [1] BORDESLEY [2]

STECHFORD stoves

GARRETTS GREEN [5]

Hagley Road

A456

B1

[2] BALSALL HEATH

HARBORNE [3] toys

SMALL HEATH

Coventry Road

TYSELEY [2] [5] [2]

HAY MILLS

cars ACOCKS GREEN

AIRPORT

A45

WOODGATE [5] aluminium alloys

precision instruments, heavy engineering

guns, motor cycles, cars

electrical goods

HALL GREEN [2]

Warwick Road

A41

SELLY OAK guns, metal, cardboard boxes [2]

BOURNVILLE [3] chocolate

Alcester Road

Stratford Road A34

Bristol Road

KING'S NORTON [5]

0   3km
0   2 miles

LONGBRIDGE [3] cars

Redditch Road

A441

A38

A43

[1]	Established by early 19th century. J, Jewellery G, Guns (now demolished) B, Brass MM, Mixed Metals
[2]	Established in second half of 19th century
[3]	Single site
[4]	Tame Valley Industrial Belt (see Fig. 6.11)
[5]	Industrial Estate

Motorway   ---- Boundary of Birmingham
Main road

6.3 Main factory areas in Birmingham

6.4 British hallmarks. Gold (*left*), silver (*right*)

Maker's mark   Standard mark   Assay Office mark   Date letter

Maker's mark   Assay Office mark   Standard mark   Date letter

the work, perhaps making rings, or setting precious stones, or engraving. These men often occupy rooms as workshops in the same old house and can easily pass on articles from one to another. Many jobs are done by outworkers. The heart of the jewellery quarter is in the jumble of nineteenth-century houses between Vyse Street, Frederick Street, St Paul's Square and Great Hampton Street (Fig. 6.5). By reading the key to this map, you can follow the movement of the industry out from the City Centre at Colmore Row.

The specialisation and smallness of the firms, and the use of houses as workshops, have been mentioned. Many of the houses and factories (see 5 on Fig. 6.5) are dilapidated and between 100 and 150 years old. The City has bought much of the land and redevelopment is proceeding rapidly. As the old houses are knocked down, arrangements are made for many of the small firms to move into the Flatted Factory, FF on Fig. 6.5. The rent of a unit in the factory is higher than for one room in an old house. This is leading to another change in the industry, as small firms are amalgamating to cut costs. To face increasing competition from the U.S.A. and Europe, some firms are replacing old premises with new factories. Payton Pepper and Sons Ltd, located at P on Fig. 6.5 and founded in 1849, is an example of this change. The new building has been designed to make the best use of the craftsman's skill. For instance, small goods are carried round the building from workman to workman at high speed by use of pneumatic air tubes; glass in the roof lets in the north light which is essential for fine, close work; there is the latest diamond-cutting machinery; and, most important, a canteen. The buildings and in some places the road pattern are altering in the centre of the jewellery quarter, but most of the firms intend to remain in the quarter.

The gun quarter has been demolished to make way for the inner ring road and the firms are scattered. In contrast, many small firms still make brass and metal goods in premises on the early sites.

6.5 The jewellery quarter

6.6 Selly Oak (1904). This is an example of an industrial area developed in the late nineteenth century at the meeting of canals, railway and road in a former village.

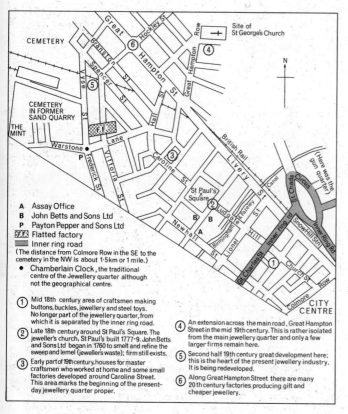

A Assay Office
B John Betts and Sons Ltd
P Payton Pepper and Sons Ltd
▨ Flatted factory
▬ Inner ring road
(The distance from Colmore Row in the SE to the cemetery in the NW is about 1·5km or 1 mile.)
● Chamberlain Clock, the traditional centre of the Jewellery quarter although not the geographical centre.

① Mid 18th century area of craftsmen making buttons, buckles, jewellery and steel toys. No longer part of the jewellery quarter, from which it is separated by the inner ring road.
② Late 18th century around St Paul's Square. The jeweller's church, St Paul's built 1777-9. John Betts and Sons Ltd began in 1760 to smelt and refine the sweep and lemel (jeweller's waste); firm still exists.
③ Early part of 19th century, houses for master craftsmen who worked at home and some small factories developed around Caroline Street. This area marks the beginning of the present-day jewellery quarter proper.
④ An extension across the main road, Great Hampton Street in the mid 19th century. This is rather isolated from the main jewellery quarter and only a few larger firms remain here.
⑤ Second half 19th century great development here; this is the heart of the present jewellery industry. It is being redeveloped.
⑥ Along Great Hampton Street there are many 20th century factories producing gilt and cheaper jewellery.

Canal
Railway
Road
Tramway
Houses built by 1904

0   1km
0   ½ mile

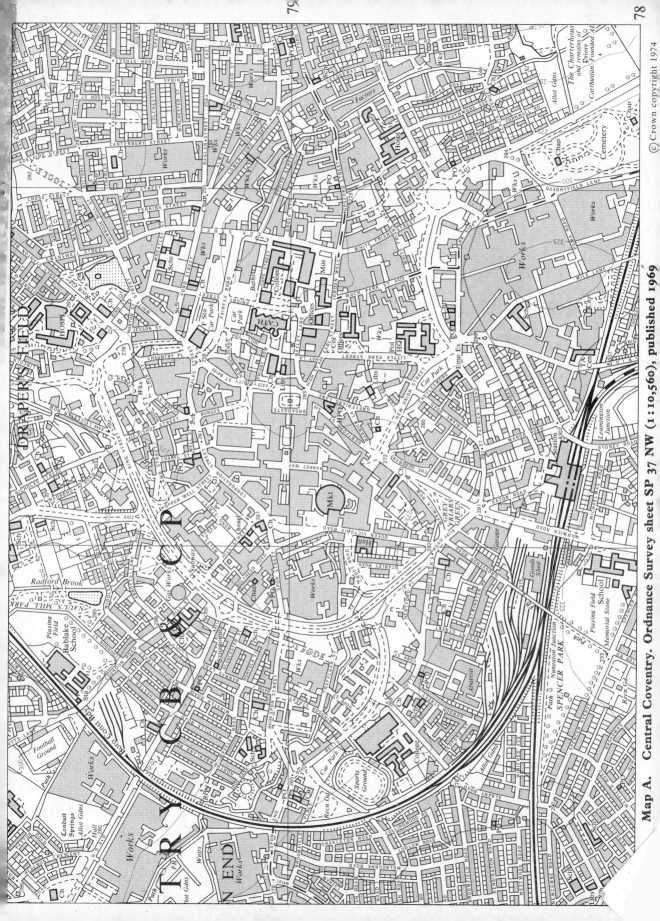

Map A.   Central Coventry. Ordnance Survey sheet SP 37 NW (1 : 10,560), published 1969

© Crown copyright 1974

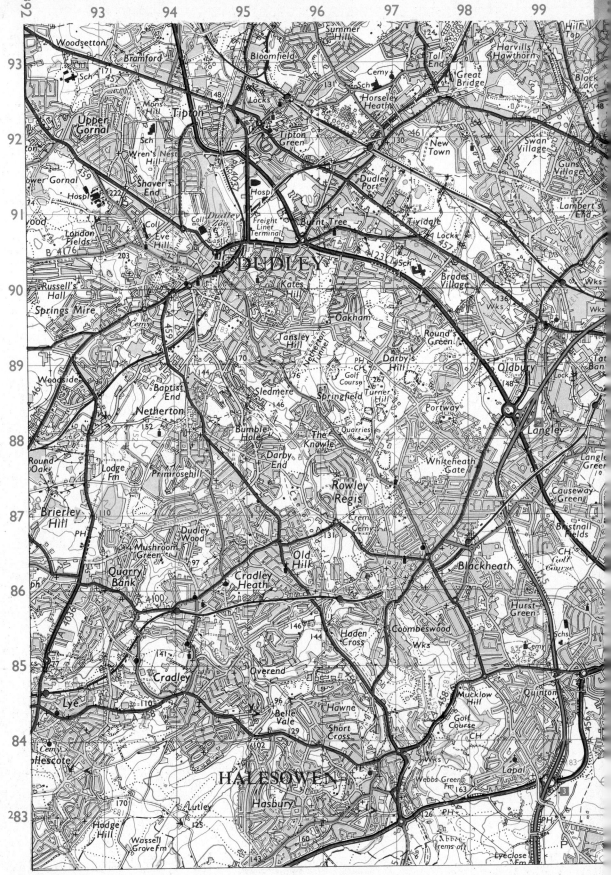

Map B.1.   The southern part of the Black Country. O.S. sheet 139 (1:50,000), 1974

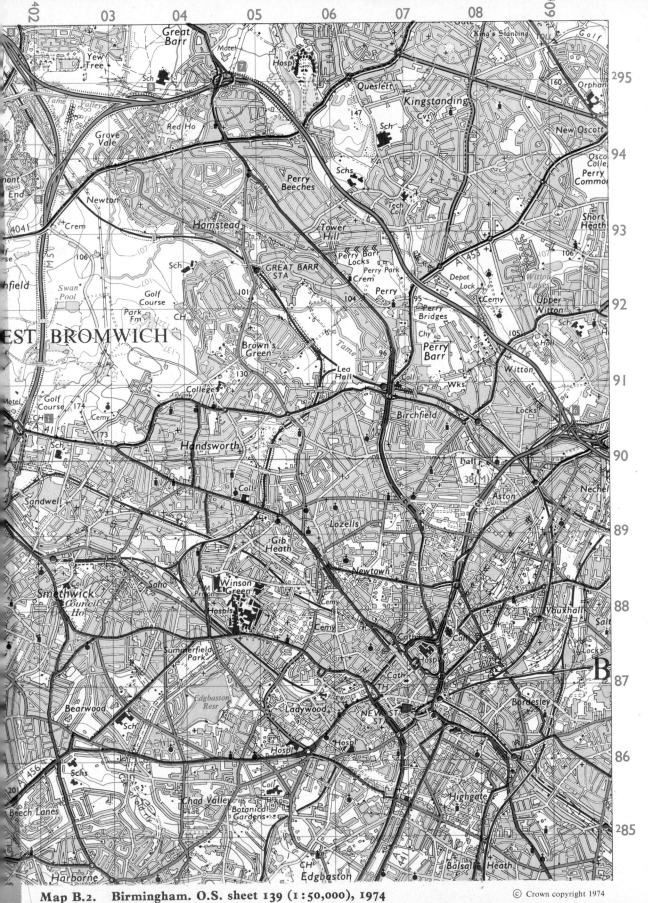

Map B.2.   Birmingham. O.S. sheet 139 (1:50,000), 1974

© Crown copyright 1974

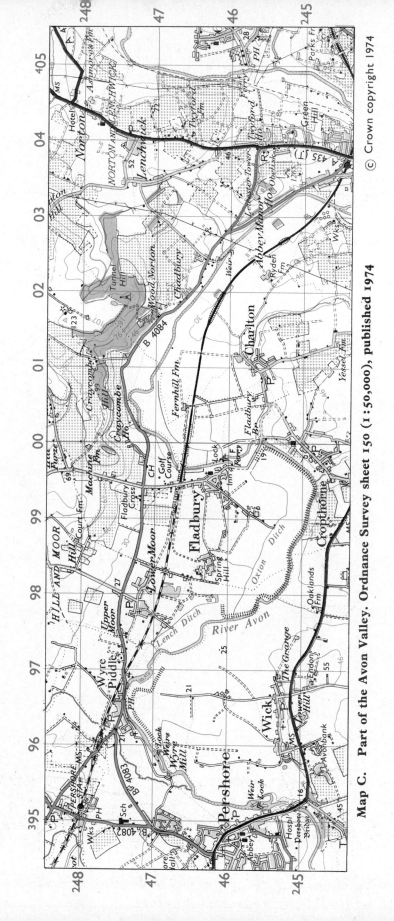

Map C. Part of the Avon Valley. Ordnance Survey sheet 150 (1:50,000), published 1974

© Crown copyright 1974

6.7 Cadbury's, Bournville (1968)

2. Industrial pockets

About 3 to 4 miles (4.8 to 6.4 km) from the City Centre is a ring of industrial pockets, marked 2 on Fig. 6.3. Some developed on the edge of nineteenth-century Birmingham, others in villages and rural areas outside. In 1911, when Greater Birmingham was formed, they became part of the city (Fig. 6.2). At first these pockets were concerned with the electrical and cycle trades and later with vehicles and machine tools. The areas included Ladywood, Balsall Heath, Selly Oak, Small Heath, Hay Mills, Aston and Saltley.

An industrial pocket at Selly Oak. Fig. 6.6 brings out the main reason why factories were built in the village of Selly Oak. Canals, a railway line and a road met here. At first raw materials were brought by water and later by railway. Copper and enamel works were built near the canal wharves and railway sidings. Workers used the tramway along the Bristol Road from Birmingham to travel to work until

houses were erected near the factories. Here is a list of some of the changes which had taken place by 1971.

   (i) The Dudley Canal is derelict.

  (ii) The Worcester and Birmingham Canal is a cruiseway and no longer a commercial canal.

 (iii) The railway station is closed for goods, but open for commuter traffic.

 (iv) The cycle factory is used by a cardboard manufacturer.

  (v) The gun and rifle factory now also makes precision instruments.

 (vi) Elliott's copper works have been taken over by a number of light engineering firms.

 (vii) The enamel works are no longer in use.

(viii) Selly Oak forms part of Birmingham.

Draw a map similar to Fig. 6.6, inserting the canals, railway, roads and outline of the works. Then label it to show the changes listed above. For example, instead of DUDLEY CANAL write DERELICT DUDLEY CANAL. Your map will tell you that it is still a factory area but that some of the buildings are used by different industries. The canals and railways are no longer important, but you have learned already that road and freightliner transport is now used by industry in Birmingham today.

3. Single factory sites
Elsewhere individual factory sites developed, marked 3 on Fig. 6.3. Two examples are the manufacture of Cadbury's chocolate at Bournville and Austin cars at Longbridge.

Bournville. Fig. 6.7 is a photograph of Cadbury's of Bournville in 1968. The buildings show three stages in the growth of the factory. The tall one is post-war, to its left beyond the tree is an inter-war building, and to its right, half hidden, is the gable end of an early twentieth-century building. An even earlier Bournville factory appears on the Ordnance Survey map for 1885. It was a good site, in a sheltered valley near canal, railway and road (Fig. 6.8).

6.8 Advantages of the site of the Bournville factory opened in 1879 (based on 1885 6″ O.S. map)

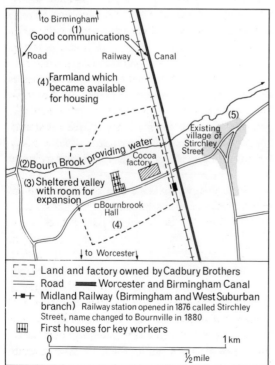

The founder of the Cadbury chocolate firm was John Cadbury. At his shop in Bull Street in the centre of Birmingham he sold tea, coffee and a little cocoa and chocolate for which he roasted the cocoa beans. This was in 1824. As the demand for cocoa and chocolate increased, he rented a factory nearby, took his brother as partner, and the firm became Cadbury Brothers. Two of his sons were responsible for moving the firm out to the country. By the late 1870s the Bridge Street factory, which had replaced the earlier one in Crooked Lane, had become too small for the fast-developing trade. It was then that more than 14½ acres (5.9 hectares) of the Bournbrook Estate, 4 miles (6.4 km) south-west of Birmingham, were purchased. On part of this land a factory was built. Its site is shown on Fig. 6.8.

Notice the name Cocoa Factory. Why was it called this? Originally cocoa and chocolate were for drinking only. Just before moving to Bournville, the firm had perfected the manufacture of a pure cocoa essence. This provided them with a beverage to market and also a supply of cocoa butter not required in the cocoa essence, which could be used to manufacture eating chocolate. Soon the cocoa and chocolate were being sold nationwide and overseas.

By 1969 the Cadbury Group of Companies had factories in Australia, Canada, New Zealand, Ireland, South Africa, Kenya, Nigeria, Ghana and India. It included the confectionery firms of J. S. Fry and Sons Ltd, James Pascall Ltd and R. S. McColl. Products such as dried milk (Marvel), instant potato (Smash) and cakes were made at subsidiary factories elsewhere. A member of the Cadbury family had been head of the firm from its beginning. This changed in 1969 when the firm merged with Schweppes Ltd. The Cadbury–Schweppes Group is an international food group with an annual turnover of more than £250,000,000.

It was unusual to build a factory in rural surroundings and it was more remarkable to build a village around it. Bournville became one of the first garden estates in the country. The idea was George Cadbury's, who proved that good houses at low rents could be built for workers. In 1900 he founded the Bournville Village Trust, which continued to build houses, schools, halls and

6.9 Car assembly line: British Leyland, Longbridge

churches around wide roads and open spaces. A worker need not be a Cadbury employee to live on the estate. The estate and house lay-out were so successful that many of the ideas were followed in the Birmingham municipal estates at a later date.

Longbridge. How many cars can you see in Fig. 6.9? Over a million have been sold; can you recognise them? This is the assembly line at Longbridge, Birmingham.

At one time or another Wolseley, B.S.A., Austin, Morris, Singer and Rover cars have been made inside the present Birmingham boundary. The largest motor manufacturing organisation in Britain is the British Leyland Motor Corporation, which includes the works making Austin, Morris, Daimler, Jaguar, Rover and Standard Triumph cars. In all, the Corporation controls 79 factories in the United Kingdom connected with vehicle assembly, car body production, engines, radiators, silencers, coach-work, foundry operations, research work and so on. In 1969 British Leyland sold 1,083,000 units

including 869,000 cars, 199,000 trucks, buses, vans and other commercial vehicles, and 15,000 agricultural tractors. Forty per cent of the total sales was overseas. Britain is a manufacturing country and must sell goods abroad to pay for raw materials and food bought from other countries. Britain tries to balance the cost of her imports against the money she earns from exports. The combination is called the national balance of payments. Vehicles are one of the main exports. British Leyland is important because practically all the components in its vehicles are British-made. By exporting 40 per cent of its production, the Corporation makes a substantial contribution to the national balance of payments.

The largest local British Leyland site covers 260 acres (105 hectares) at Longbridge, Birmingham. Here a car factory was started by Herbert Austin in 1905 in a derelict printing works 7 miles (11 km) outside Birmingham. This became the Austin Motor Company. From 237 employees making two cars a week in 1902, 22,000 people now work at the Longbridge plant and 10,000 vehicles can be turned out each week. Herbert Austin had made sure there was plenty of room to expand.

In 1970 British Leyland re-organised its factories into five groups. Longbridge is the organising centre for one of these, namely the Austin–Morris and Manufacturing Group. This Group includes factories in Birmingham, Castle Bromwich, Coventry, Oxford, Swindon and Llanelli. Between them they produce car bodies, components, carburettors, radiators, engines and silencers for the Austin–Morris vehicles. For instance at King's Norton, Bir-

mingham, the engines for the Mini, and the Austin 1100 and 1300 are made.

Bournville and Longbridge are two of the factory sites numbered 3 in the key to Fig. 6.3. In each case the former country site is now a suburb of Birmingham and the original factory has been replaced by extensive works which are part of large combines.

4. A large industrial belt

In the twentieth century the biggest expansion of industry has taken place along the Tame Valley, marked 4 on Fig. 6.3.

6.10   Aerial view of the Tame Valley

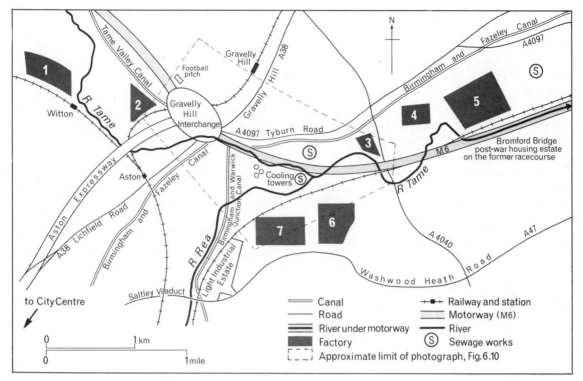

6.11 Factories and communications in the Tame Valley

Tame valley industries. Fig. 6.10 is an aerial photograph of part of the Tame Valley in north-east Birmingham. How many of the following can you spot: motorway, railway, canal, gas holder, power station, sports ground, reservoir, factory?

The 'plane taking the photograph was flying low over Gravelly Hill Interchange where the Aston Expressway from the City Centre meets the M6. The River Tame is hidden by the motorway, but its tributary the River Rea is the dark line curving between the gas holders and the cooling towers.

More of the valley is shown in Fig. 6.11. On this map the central part inside the broken line is the land covered by the photograph. To help you fix the position of the photograph in relation to the map, find the football pitch in the bottom left-hand corner. Next find the cooling towers. Pitch and towers are named on the map. Between them is the interchange. A factory is shown by the canal in the foreground of the photograph. This is one of the belt of factories along the

Tame Valley. On Fig. 6.11, some of the largest are numbered.

Factory 1:   Metals
Factory 2:   Electrical goods
Factory 3:   Steel tubes
Factory 4:   Oil heaters
Factory 5:   Tyres
Factory 6:   Car components
Factory 7:   Rolling stock, e.g. railway carriages

Between them the factories employ over 30,000 people. They benefit greatly by being near to the motorway and the interchange. Yet the factories were built long before motorways were necessary (Table 6.1). Originally the land in the valley was cheap because it was damp and poor for farming. It was not needed for housing because better drained areas were still available. There was no problem of transporting goods or workers. Wharves and stations could be built quite easily alongside the existing canals and railways. Water for use in the factories was obtained by bores into the underlying rock of sandstone and pebble beds. The motor industry was growing rapidly in other parts of Birmingham and needed the metal, tyres and electrical parts produced in the Tame Valley factories.

Read down the list of 1971 products in Table 6.1. The link with the motor industry is still there. Notice that each firm is now part of a much larger group. During the last fifty years the factory belt has extended along the valley to the east of the earlier pockets of industry at Witton, Aston and Saltley. There was cheap land and room to expand. The inter-war houses in the photograph (Fig. 6.10) were built to supply

Table 6.1 *Factories in the Tame Valley marked on Fig. 6.11*

Number on map, Fig. 6.11	Factory	Date when first factory was built in the Valley	Employees – 1971	Product – 1971	Name of Group of which factory is a member
1	Kynoch Works	1901	10,000	1. Ammunition 2. Copper and brass sheet, strip, foil, rods, wire 3. New metals such as titanium melted & forged 4. Components, e.g. motorcycle carburettors 5. Foreign coins 6. Zip fasteners	Imperial Metal Industries
2	G.E.C.	1899	3,400 (on the site)	1. Heavylift electro-magnets 2. Plastic mouldings 3. Lamp and fittings depot	The General Electric Company Limited
3	Bromford Tubeworks	1917	1,000	1. Carbon alloy and stainless steel tubes	British Steel Corporation
4	Valor Company Ltd	1924		1. Oil and gas heaters 2. Heater cases for British Leyland 1971 Marina Car	Valor Group of Companies
5	Fort Dunlop	1919	10,000	1. Tyres and tubes 2. Chemical products, e.g. adhesives, paint materials, sealants 3. Research in new materials and processes	Dunlop Group
6	British Leyland Ward End Transmission Plant		4,400	Front suspension and rear axle units for Austin Morris cars and vans	British Leyland
7	Metro Cammell Ltd	1909	1,850	Railway coaches. Wagons for oil products and cement	Cammell – Laird

homes for the increased numbers of work-people. Chapter 4 described the acute need for housing land in Birmingham today. On the disused racecourse at Bromford Bridge is one of the five post-war housing estates. The Tame Valley zone is the most heavily industrialised sector in modern Birmingham.

5. Industrial estates

As Birmingham spread outwards before the Second World War, further works connected with vehicles, metals and machinery were built at Hall Green, Acocks Green and Stechford. A new development was an industrial estate where land was given over solely to factory and warehouse buildings.

King's Norton factory centre. This was the first local industrial estate. More than fifty manufacturers employ about 4,000 people. Six of the firms describe their work as follows:

Anderton and Clift. Manufacturers and designers of jigs, tools fixtures, suppliers of engineering and factory requirements.

Barworth Steel Sales Ltd. Manufacturers of high grade tool and alloy steel.

Cameron Price Ltd. Precision industrial mouldings, design and development in plastic.

Deritend Tinning Ltd. Tinners.

Guest, John (Nuts and Bolts) Ltd. Manufacturers of bright steel nuts for automobile, cycle and electrical industries.

King's Norton Tube Co. Ltd. Brass and copper tubes.

Most of the firms are making light engineering products. The majority of the factories are single-storey and are supplied with gas, water and electricity. They were built by the Slough Estate Group of Companies which bought the 55 acres (22 hectares) of land with some old factories in 1931. A purpose-built factory which could be rented by a manufacturer was quite a new idea at that time. The Company's first factory estate was at Slough, and today it has others in Canada, Australia, Belgium, Germany and Japan.

Garretts Green industrial estate. This is a corporation estate belonging to the City of Birmingham. It was started in 1950 on part of some farmland bought for a housing estate. This differs from the factory centre at King's Norton in many ways:

   (i) The land can be bought or leased.

   (ii) There are many warehouses as well as factories.

   (iii) Firms build their own factories or warehouses.

   (iv) The estate contains some food factories, for example, a bakery and a sausage factory.

   (v) Some plots of land are retained for firms displaced by redevelopment schemes in the city.

Industrial estates are being built near the motorways as the demand for warehouses increases; the one at Saltley (Fig. 6.3) is an example.

Some of the factories grew up around canal and rail transport. Now the raw materials and finished goods are carried along roads. On Fig. 6.3, the different types of factory areas are shown in relation to the main roads and motorways.

Exercises   1. What changes are taking place in the jewellery industry in Birmingham? Give reasons for these changes.

           2. Why was industry attracted to the village of Selly Oak?

           3. (*a*) What were the advantages of the Bournville site when it was developed in 1879?

               (*b*) Bournville was a factory in a garden with houses for the workers. Where else in Britain were factories built on similar lines?

4. The Austin–Morris Group is one of the five groups in British Leyland. What are the other four? What other major motor manufacturing companies are there in Britain?
5. Fig. 5.17 and Fig. 6.10 show the Gravelly Hill Interchange. How do the two photographs differ?
6. (a) List the land uses shown in Fig. 6.10. Put them in the following groups: communications, industrial uses, housing, farming, recreation.
   (b) Choose one group. Draw a sketch from Fig. 6.10 to show, by labelling or a key, the location of the land use in that group.
7. There are about 350,000 workers in Birmingham's manufacturing industries. What percentage of these work in the seven factories in the Tame Valley?
8. For what reasons has the Tame Valley been used as the site for a motorway?
9. Why do firms merge together into large companies? Give examples of this kind of merger.
10. Draw a sketch-map to show the site of Fort Dunlop in relation to the River Tame and communications.
11. What part did these men play in the growth of Birmingham's industry: James Watt, Matthew Boulton, William Murdoch, George Cadbury (son of John Cadbury), Herbert Austin?
12. The following percentages are for employees in manufacturing industry in Birmingham for 1952:

	%
Food, drink and tobacco	7.4
Chemicals and allied industries	3.5
Metal manufacturing	7.6
Engineering and electrical goods	22.5
Vehicles	24.6
Metal goods not elsewhere specified	20.5
Paper, printing and publishing	3.2
Remainder	10.7

(a) Construct a pie graph to show the information given in the above table (show 1% by an angle of 3.6°).
(b) In what way is your pie graph different from Fig. 6.1?
(c) Complete the table below to show increases or decreases in the different categories by 1969.

By 1969

Increase	Decrease
Metal manufacturing	Food, drink and tobacco

(d) Give reasons to explain the decline in the number of employees in: (i) the chemical industry; (ii) vehicles.

7 | THE BLACK COUNTRY

7.1   The Dudley arms

In the centre of the Dudley arms (Fig. 7.1) are represented an anchor, a trilobite and a miner's Davy lamp. The anchor refers to the iron trade, the fossil (Fig. 2.2) to the limestone quarries and the lamp to the collieries. The Black Country towns, of which Dudley is one, developed because of rich deposits of iron, limestone and coal. The Black Country is a distinct region with two main characteristics:

1. its inhabitants have a remarkable dialect with its own words, phrases and intonation;
2. it developed as a centre for the production and manufacture of iron, and has changed into a centre of the metal trades, producing various metals and manufacturing a great variety of metal goods.

Look back at Fig. 2.7 and you will notice that the Black Country straddles the Ridge, which divides it into two parts, the Tame Valley and the Stour Valley. It stretches roughly 8 miles (12.8 km) from north to south and 10 miles (16 km) from east to west.

Before the eighteenth century there were iron-smelting settlements in these valleys. The local iron and limestone were smelted with charcoal. Later the whole area became industrialised because of (i) the use of coal for smelting, (ii) the invention of the steam engine, (iii) the digging of canals. In South Staffordshire there was a rich 30-ft (9-m) coal seam, excellent for use in furnaces. The steam engine was used to pump water from the collieries and to drive machinery in furnaces and factories. The canal transport provided the means of exporting the iron products and coal. A jumble of collieries, quarries, furnaces and houses spread across the Ridge. The coal was dug and mined where it outcropped, and industrial settlements developed. These included Wednesbury, Darlaston, Willenhall, Bilston, Bradley, Coseley, Tipton, Dudley, Netherton, Brierley Hill, Rowley Regis and Lye. Some of these names on the Ordnance Survey extract (Map B.1) will help you locate the Black Country. The coal seams continued, concealed below younger rocks, to Oldbury, Smethwick, West Bromwich and Halesowen. These towns form the fringe of the Black Country. Not only was pig iron produced, it was also extensively manufactured into various articles. Each town began to specialise in a particular branch of the iron industry. For example:

Light manufactures	Willenhall	– Locks
	Wednesfield	– Keys
Heavy manufactures	Wednesbury	– Tubes and springs
	Cradley and Netherton	– Chains and anchors
	Tipton	– Structural iron work
	Bilston	– Heavy forgings

These products are known as hardware.

Coneygre Foundry, Tipton (Fig. 7.2), is an example of the continuity of the iron industry.

As long ago as 1291 iron was worked here, using charcoal for processing. In the eighteenth century, ironstone, coal, fireclay and limestone were mined at shallow depths. The thick 30-ft (9-m) coal seam ran through the property. Throughout the nineteenth century pig iron was produced from blast furnaces which were pulled down in 1896.

Today a fully mechanised foundry turns out iron castings, particularly for the car industry. The workmen live locally as in the past. To survive, the industry had to change. Pig iron is no longer produced as the local minerals are exhausted. Castings are made instead. For these pig iron, sand and other raw materials are brought in from abroad as well as from Britain (Fig. 7.2). A lorry which can go to any part of the works is more efficient than a canal boat or railway truck. So the canal and railway sidings are no longer used. Finally the foundry has become a member of a much larger concern, the Birmid Industries Group.

Fig. 7.3 gives details of employment for certain Black Country and adjacent towns in 1964. The areas of the circles represent the total number of employed persons in the towns. The segments of the circles indicate the separate industries. It is clear that metal manufacture, metal goods and engineering dominate the manufacturing industries. In Wednesbury, which many consider to be the heart of the Black Country, these three industries employ 66 per cent of the workers. As the iron smelting declined with the exhaustion of the minerals, production of and working in a variety of metals took its place. In the early twentieth century,

7.2   Coneygre Foundry (SO 960913)   **7.3**   (*opposite page*) **Insured employees (1964)**

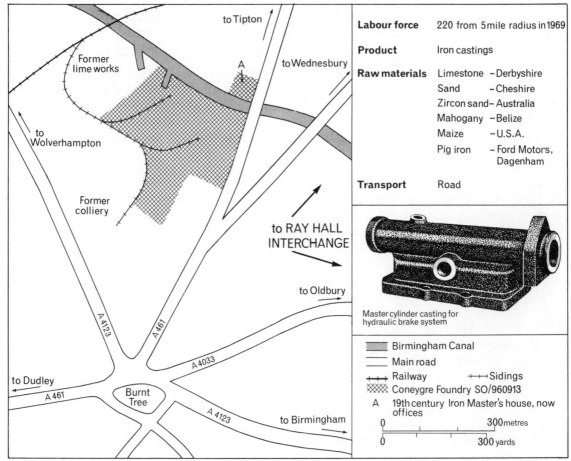

Labour force	220 from 5 mile radius in 1969
Product	Iron castings
Raw materials	Limestone – Derbyshire
	Sand – Cheshire
	Zircon sand – Australia
	Mahogany – Belize
	Maize – U.S.A.
	Pig iron – Ford Motors, Dagenham
Transport	Road

Master cylinder casting for hydraulic brake system

Birmingham Canal
Main road
Railway   Sidings
Coneygre Foundry SO/960913
A   19th century Iron Master's house, now offices

0   300 metres
0   300 yards

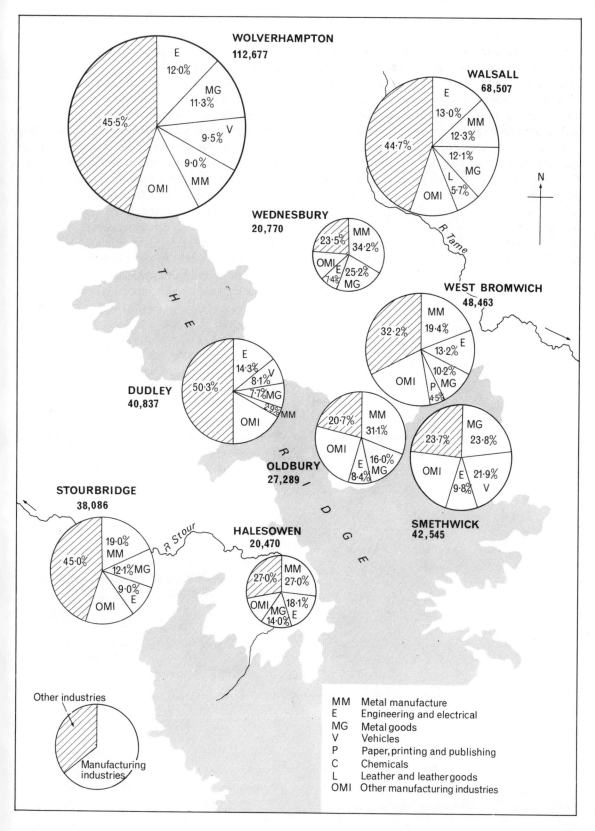

WOLVERHAMPTON
112,677

E 12·0%
MG 11·3%
V 9·5%
MM 9·0%
OMI
45·5%

WALSALL
68,507

E 13·0%
MM 12·3%
MG 12·1%
L 5·7%
OMI
44·7%

WEDNESBURY
20,770

MM 34·2%
MG 25·2%
E 7·4%
OMI
23·5%

WEST BROMWICH
48,463

MM 19·4%
E 13·2%
MG 10·2%
P 4·5%
OMI
32·2%

DUDLEY
40,837

E 14·3%
V 8·1%
MG 7·7%
MM 2·9%
OMI
50·3%

OLDBURY
27,289

MM 31·1%
MG 16·0%
E 8·4%
OMI
20·7%

SMETHWICK
42,545

MG 23·8%
V 21·9%
E 9·8%
OMI
23·7%

STOURBRIDGE
38,086

MM 19·0%
MG 12·1%
E 9·0%
OMI
45·0%

HALESOWEN
20,470

MM 27·0%
E 18·1%
MG 14·0%
OMI
27·0%

R Tame

R Stour

T H E   R I D G E

N

Other industries

Manufacturing industries

MM   Metal manufacture
E   Engineering and electrical
MG   Metal goods
V   Vehicles
P   Paper, printing and publishing
C   Chemicals
L   Leather and leather goods
OMI   Other manufacturing industries

manufacturers with an ample supply of skilled metal workers were able to make parts and accessories for the new cycle and motor trades.

The 1964 figures were chosen for Fig. 7.3 because soon after this date the Black Country towns lost their separate identity. In 1966, new boundaries were drawn: Walsall, Wolverhampton and the Black Country towns were regrouped into the following five county boroughs:

Dudley (181,380): Dudley, Brierley Hillm most of Sedgley and Coseley, parts of Tipton and Amblecote.

Walsall (184,060): Walsall, Willenhall, Darlaston, parts of Wednesbury and Bilston.

Warley (169,440): Smethwick, Oldbury, Rowley Regis.

West Bromwich (166,626): West Bromwich, Tipton, Wednesbury, parts of Darlaston and Coseley.

Wolverhampton (265,000): Wolverhampton, Coseley, most of Bilston, Wednesfield and Tettenhall, parts of Sedgley and Willenhall.

Check these on Fig. 7.4. Stourbridge and Halesowen were not included and remained municipal boroughs in Worcestershire.

The metal trade employs large numbers of men in all these boroughs. Metal is refined and smelted, and made into many products. Some of

7.4   The five county boroughs (1966)

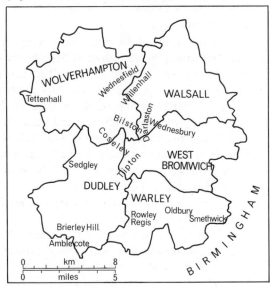

them are: heavy engineering castings, tubes in steel, brass and copper, forgings, chains, nuts and bolts, machine tools, electrical apparatus, car and aircraft components.

Two more old-established industries are glass and chemicals, both connected with the South Staffordshire coalfield.

Coal seams rest on clay which contained the roots of the plants and trees from which the coal seams formed. This is called fireclay and makes excellent glasshouse pots and firebricks for furnaces which will withstand great heat. The glass industry is located at Brierley Hill, Amblecote and Stourbridge, where a belt of fireclay existed.

The world's first two ships specially made to carry phosphorus, *Albright Pioneer* and *Albright Explorer*, bring phosphorus from Newfoundland to Portishead Dock at the mouth of the Bristol Avon. Some of it is taken by special road tanker to the Oldbury factory of Albright and Wilson Ltd, to be converted into phosphoric acid, a wide range of phosphates and other phosphorus-based chemicals. In one form or another, these products are used in rust-proofing solutions, toothpaste, metal cleaning and polishing, fire extinguishers, antibiotics, crease-resistant finishes, activated carbon for sugar refining, detergents, wool dyeing, water softeners, penicillin manufacture, insecticides, catalysts, matches, plastic chemicals.

At one time phosphorus was made from bone ash. By 1851 Arthur Albright, a Quaker, had built a furnace at Oldbury for producing phosphates from phosphate rock for the match industry. He exhibited at the Great Exhibition at Crystal Palace, London. Albright chose to build the factory at Oldbury because an existing alkali works could provide cheap acid; there was a local supply of coal for the furnace, fireclay for the making of retorts, clay for building bricks; the main Birmingham Canal linked Oldbury to the ports as well as Birmingham and other parts of the Black Country. Today there is no phosphorus furnace at Oldbury, although it closed only recently. The furnace is some thousands of miles away at Long Harbour in Newfoundland. It is in a modern plant owned by Albright and Wilson Ltd. This site was chosen with as much care as Arthur Albright chose the first one at

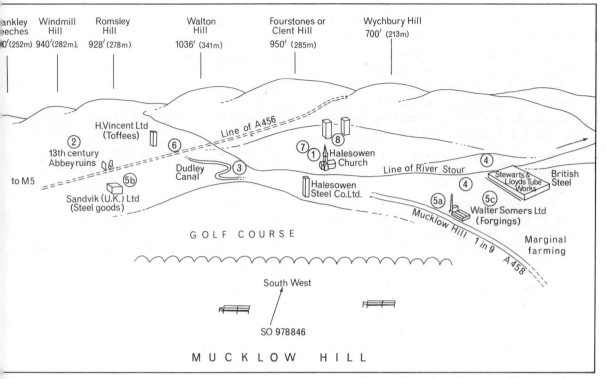

ankley
eeches
0'(252m)

Windmill
Hill
940'(282m)

Romsley
Hill
928' (278m)

Walton
Hill
1036' (341m)

Fourstones or
Clent Hill
950' (285m)

Wychbury Hill
700' (213m)

H. Vincent Ltd
(Toffees)

Line of A 456

②

13th century
Abbey ruins

⑥

⑦ ① Halesowen
⑧ Church

Line of River Stour

④

Dudley
Canal

③

to M5

⑤b

Halesowen
Steel Co. Ltd.

④

Stewarts &
Lloyds Tube
Works

British
Steel

Sandvik (U.K.) Ltd
(Steel goods)

⑤a

⑤c

Walter Somers Ltd
(Forgings)

Mucklow Hill 1 in 9   A 458

Marginal
farming

G O L F   C O U R S E

South West

SO 978846

M U C K L O W   H I L L

7.5   Sketch looking west over Halesowen

Oldbury. At Long Harbour there is abundant cheap electricity, and a phosphorus furnace uses a great deal. The phosphate rock, which is imported by sea from Florida, has a much shorter journey than to Oldbury. The Newfoundland Government provides roads, water and housing. The harbour is deep and ice-free and on the sea lanes between England and North America. So it is cheaper to produce the phosphorus in Newfoundland and transport it to England in the two tankers.

The original founder factory at Oldbury is now part of Albright and Wilson Ltd, an international organisation with headquarters in London. This organization is made up of eight divisions, one of which is the Oldbury division. The manufacture of phosphorus-based chemicals is the main production in the Oldbury division. This is carried on in factories which employ 3,200 people at Rainham, Letchworth, Stratford (London), Portishead, Kirkby, Widnes and Oldbury. Increasingly, other chemicals which do not contain phosphorus are being made in the Old-

bury division. For example, it is the largest producer in Europe of aluminium salts, which are used in certain cosmetics.

Halesowen: a town on the fringe of the Black Country

Fig. 7.5 is a sketch of the landscape looking west over Halesowen to the Clent Hills. The viewpoint, SO 978846, is on Mucklow Hill at the narrowing of the Ridge (Fig. 2.1). Halesowen lies in the Stour Valley at the southern edge of the South Staffordshire coalfield, and coal was mined until the 1960s. From Mucklow Hill it is possible to see quite clearly features which tell us about stages in the growth of Halesowen. These are numbered on Fig. 7.5:

1. The site of a Saxon settlement and the later Norman church.
2. The ruins of the thirteenth-century abbey.
3. A remaining stretch of the eighteenth-century canal.
4. The site of disused collieries.

61

5. Industrial areas: (*a*) the old, (*b*) post-war, (*c*) proposed.
6. The A456, a feeder road to the M5, which by-passes Central Halesowen.
7. Redevelopment in the town centre.
8. New housing estates.

We learn from the Domesday Book that there was a Saxon village in Halesowen. Probably between 200 and 300 people lived and worked on the land in the Stour Valley. Although the Saxon church has gone, parts of the Norman one which replaced it remain in the present church. In the thirteenth century, the building of an abbey on the banks of the Stour brought learned monks into the area. It was an abbot who obtained the charter for a weekly market and an October fair. Halesowen became a small market town. As well as being concerned with farming and trading, Halesowen men were working in iron by the eighteenth century. It became one of the small industrial valley settlements mentioned earlier in the chapter. Along the Stour were furnaces where iron was smelted with the use of charcoal. From the furnace the cast iron was taken to the forge where it was hammered into wrought iron. Wrought nails were made in their thousands in small nail shops attached to the nailers' houses. This was a domestic industry which survived on a small scale until recently.

The road to Birmingham was very rough and steep for horses and carts carrying away the iron products. Eventually a turnpike road was made in 1753 up Mucklow Hill (Fig. 7.6). In the first instance industry had centred around the River Stour, but with the cutting of a canal and later the building of a railway line, factories grew up alongside the canal and railway. Now, with the return to road transport, the new factories are built on the feeder roads to the motorway.

Even so, the site of many present-day factories dates back to the canal period. Two examples are marked on Fig. 7.6, a tube works and a forge.

Coombs Wood Tube Works, Halesowen

At Coombs Wood, tubes which have been made at Corby in Northamptonshire are cut into required sections and protected with plastic. In this latter process, colour is added. Grey tubes are for transport signs, brown for oil companies, yellow for gas pipes, black for the Post Office. The works are part of the Tubes Division of the British Steel Corporation, which was formed by the British Government when it nationalised most of the steel industry in July 1967. There are other local tube works in this division at Birmingham, Wednesbury and Wolverhampton.

Tube-making at Coombs Wood started in 1860 when Abraham Barnsley set up as a 'Patent Tube Manufacturer for Gas, Electric, Steam and Bedstead Purposes'. The works occupied an acre (0.4 hectare) on the east side of the canal, quite near to Mucklow Hill. Later, by the amalgamation of Scottish and English tube-making concerns, it became Stewarts and Lloyds. Most companies taken over by the British Steel Corporation no longer trade under their old names so this is known as Coombs Wood Tube Works. It is a large 56-acre (22.4 hectare) site stretching along both sides of the canal.

7.6 Communications which in turn have helped Halesowen's industries

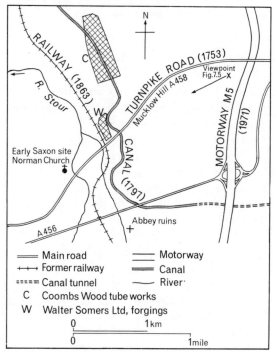

Legend:
- ════ Main road
- ════ Motorway
- ┿━┿ Former railway
- ──── Canal
- ═════ Canal tunnel
- ──── River
- C Coombs Wood tube works
- W Walter Somers Ltd, forgings

0 — 1 km
0 — 1 mile

7.7 (*opposite page*) **Field record of a walk down Mucklow Hill into Halesowen town centre**

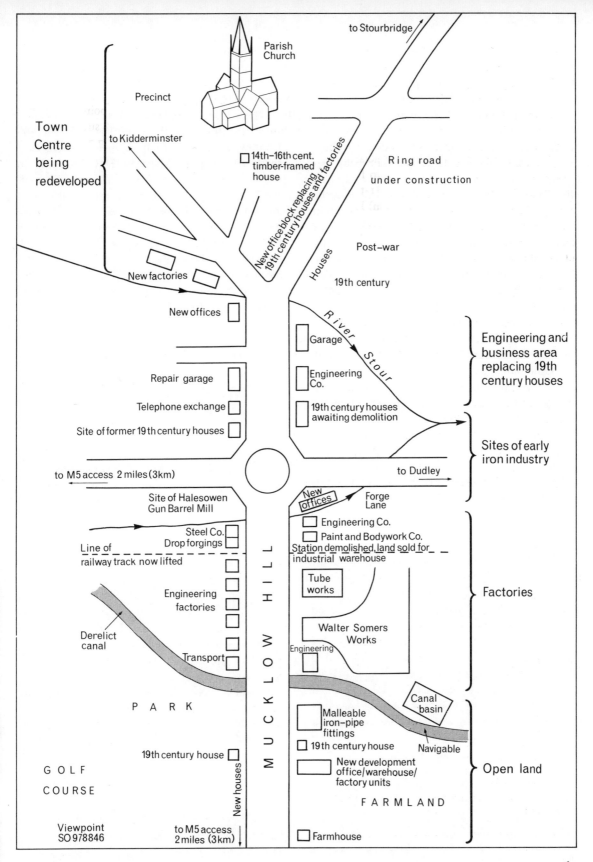

to Stourbridge

Parish Church

Precinct

Town Centre being redeveloped

to Kidderminster

14th–16th cent. timber-framed house

New office block replacing 19th century houses and factories

Ring road under construction

Post-war

Houses

19th century

New factories

New offices

River Stour

Garage

Engineering Co.

19th century houses awaiting demolition

Engineering and business area replacing 19th century houses

Repair garage

Telephone exchange

Site of former 19th century houses

Sites of early iron industry

to M5 access 2 miles (3km)

to Dudley

New offices

Forge Lane

Site of Halesowen Gun Barrel Mill

Steel Co. Drop forgings

Engineering Co.

Paint and Bodywork Co.

Station demolished, land sold for industrial warehouse

Line of railway track now lifted

M U C K L O W   H I L L

Tube works

Engineering factories

Walter Somers Works

Factories

Derelict canal

Engineering

Transport

P A R K

Canal basin

Malleable iron-pipe fittings

19th century house

Navigable

19th century house

New houses

New development office/warehouse/factory units

Open land

G O L F   C O U R S E

F A R M L A N D

Viewpoint SO 978846

to M5 access 2 miles (3km)

Farmhouse

63

Walter Somers Ltd, Haywood Forge, Halesowen

Less than half a mile (0.8 km) away from the early tube works, a forge on Mucklow Hill was turning out wrought-iron anchors and chains. In 1866 Walter Somers bought the forge and introduced steam hammers for heavier forgings. He obtained contracts to supply the Admiralty. Today there are two forges. The heavy one can handle an 80-ton (81-tonne) ingot. Marine shafts up to 65 feet (20 m) long, and huge crankshafts weighing up to 160 tons (162 tonnes) can be produced. The light forge turns out rings, rims, shafts and bars under 2 tons (2 tonnes) in weight.

Walter Somers Ltd is Europe's largest die-block manufacturer. Special steels are used to make a master block or pattern which is known as a die. These are used in the metal and plastic industries. The firm amalgamated with a Manchester concern to form the Mitchell Somers Group of Companies.

The chief industries in Halesowen are still those related to iron and steel, such as weldless tube, stainless steel, anchors, nuts and bolts and foundry work. A newer one is lens-making and an interesting survival is the horn button industry.

As in the canal and railway era, Halesowen is undergoing a period of expansion. The population has risen from 40,900 in 1951 to 53,993 in 1971. There are new small factories and many attractive housing estates. Young people can live in Halesowen and work in Birmingham. It started earlier than neighbouring towns to modernise the centre of the town. Houses and flats were built on open land near the church. Shopping facilities were inadequate, so a pedestrian precinct was built on and around the old market site. Plenty of free car-parking space and a Sainsbury's food store attract shoppers from West Birmingham as well as from Halesowen and surrounding areas. The town library recently built in the precinct encourages a constant flow of people past the shops. The town centre is small enough to enable the old winding streets to be maintained and some to be made traffic-free. A plan released in 1971 shows a ring road which will take much of the traffic.

Halesowen separates two contrasting areas. To the north lies the heavily industrialised Black Country, whilst to the south is the Green Belt. The rebuilding has given Halesowen a lively atmosphere, rather like that of a busy market town.

A walk from the viewpoint on Mucklow Hill to the church is a good summary of past and present Halesowen. Fig. 7.7 is a fair copy of a field record made on such a walk.

Dotted over the Black Country are pockets of uneven land where quarries and mines were worked. The need for building-land is so great that these are being cleared, levelled and left to settle. Later, the sites are used for recreation grounds, houses, schools and industrial estates. Halesowen provides one of many examples. Fig. 7.8 is a sketch drawn from the 1955 Ordnance Survey map. It shows an area which was once

7.8 A changing landscape (based on O.S. SO 98 SE)

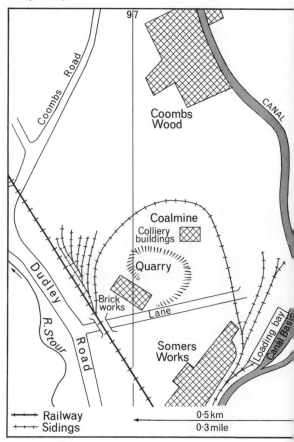

very busy. Clay was dug from the quarry for brick-making, coal was brought up the mine, trucks and passenger trains ran on the railway line, narrow-boats carried iron and coal on the canal. Goods were transferred from the canal basin to the railway loading bay. By 1970, Fig. 7.8 was completely out-of-date. Except for the colliery workings, all the land between Coombs Wood and Walter Somers Ltd had been levelled for an industrial estate. One of the few reminders of past land use is service roads following the route of the railway tracks.

Some of the recent changes in the Black Country have been mentioned already. One of the most interesting is that it is becoming less black. The increased use of oil, electricity, gas and smokeless fuels, instead of coal, makes the air cleaner. The dark soot-grimed factories and houses are being replaced by large glass and concrete buildings.

Exercises

1. (a) Why did the Black Country become important for iron production in the eighteenth and nineteenth centuries?
   (b) Why did iron production decline?
   (c) As iron production declined, metal manufacture increased. Name some of the metal goods manufactured today.

2. (a) Draw a grid the same size as O.S. extract, Map B.1, adding Northing line 90.
   (b) Print in the correct place the names of the Black Country towns shown.
   (c) (i) Draw a rectangle to represent the area covered by Fig. 7.2.
       (ii) In blue, mark and name River Stour.
       (iii) Shade the Ridge.
       (iv) Print boldly 'South Staffordshire Coalfield' in the correct place (check from Fig. 2.7).

3. Make a list of the Black Country towns you have marked on your map for Question 2. By each name indicate the county borough to which it has belonged since 1966.

4. Make a drawing of a blast furnace and describe how it works.

5. When did Henry Bessemer live and how did his work affect metal production?

6. Name a good viewpoint overlooking your own town or village. If the town is large, choose a suburb. Using Fig. 7.5 as a guide, sketch the main landmarks from the viewpoint. Visit these. Information on the landmarks could be followed up in reference books and from old maps.

7. Why did Halesowen develop from a small market town into an industrial centre?

8. A town guidebook is always a useful start when searching for information. What does the one for Walsall tell you about the leather industry?

9. What part have communications played in the development of the Black Country up to the present day?

8 | THE BLYTHE–TAME LOWLAND

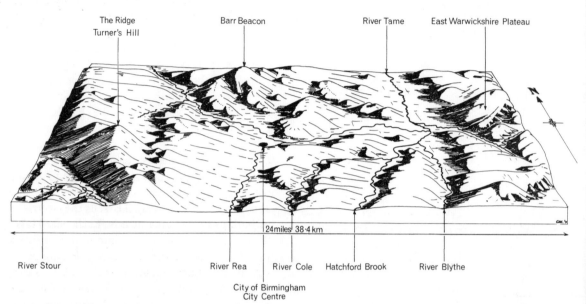

The Ridge
Turner's Hill — Barr Beacon — River Tame — East Warwickshire Plateau

N

24 miles 38·4 km

River Stour — River Rea — River Cole — Hatchford Brook — River Blythe

City of Birmingham
City Centre

8.1 Block diagram of the Tame Valley

The block diagram, Fig. 8.1, is a representation of the landscape around Birmingham. Compared with the distance on the ground (horizontal distance), the height of the land (vertical distance) has been exaggerated. The hills look higher and steeper than they are, but the scale enables them to be picked out more easily. The Ridge, Turner's Hill and the River Rea have been mentioned already. In this chapter we are looking at the land east of Birmingham.

The eastern part of the diagram shows two main relief regions. First, the wide lowland where the River Blythe meets the River Tame. Secondly, the higher land of the East Warwickshire Plateau. Both are in the Green Belt (see Fig. 4.9). There are few factories in the area and no large town, but it has become a source of energy for the West Midlands.

Energy means power from coal, gas, oil and nuclear fuel. All, except nuclear power, are obtained from this eastern part. In the last twenty

years there has been a great power revolution. Up to the 1950s coal was the main source of power, as it had been for 200 years. Coal was used in its natural form or as coke, gas and electricity.

In the 1950s coal had to compete with oil. Although the latter was imported into Britain, it was cheaper to use than coal. By 1970 oil was becoming more important than coal as a source of power. Coal and oil are now being successfully challenged by natural gas from the North Sea. The confirmation of a major oil field also under the North Sea suggests another change in the future. A British oil supply would make us less dependent on imported supplies. Throughout the last twenty years, the Blythe–Tame lowland has been involved in this energy change.

Coal: The Warwickshire Coalfield

The Warwickshire coalfield is a triangular island of coal stretching 25 miles (40 km) from Tamworth in the north to Coventry in the south

66

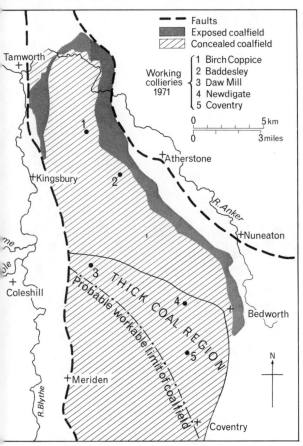

Map legend content:

- – – Faults
- Exposed coalfield
- Concealed coalfield

Working collieries 1971
1 Birch Coppice
2 Baddesley
3 Daw Mill
4 Newdigate
5 Coventry

0   5 km
0   3 miles

Tamworth
Kingsbury
Atherstone
R. Anker
Nuneaton
Coleshill
THICK COAL REGION
Probable workable limit of coalfield
Bedworth
Meriden
R. Blythe
Coventry
N

8.2   The Warwickshire coalfield

(Fig. 8.2). The first collieries were on the exposed coalfield on the eastern edge. No iron-working industry arose here as in the Black Country and the collieries remained small. As the coal in South Staffordshire became exhausted, the Warwickshire collieries expanded to sell coal to the Black Country. New deep shafts were sunk into the concealed coalfield. There are now four working collieries on the concealed coalfield. They are Birch Coppice, Baddesley, Daw Mill, Newdigate and Coventry (the last two have merged together). The newest is Daw Mill, which started production in 1965. Together they raise about 320,000 tons (325,000 tonnes), which is 3 per cent of the output of the country. The coal is used mainly in power stations; the C.E.G.B. (Central Electricity Generating Board) is the chief buyer. Coal is also processed into smokeless fuel for domestic use. It is taken by conveyor from Coventry Colliery to the adjoining National Coal Board Homefire smokeless fuel plant.

Electricity: Hams Hall power station

Cooling towers, as in Fig. 8.3, are the features you notice first about a modern power station. Large quantities of cooling water are used over and over again. Each tower is a large chimney and the white plume is water vapour carried out by the draught. The loss of water by evaporation is made up by river water. Power stations in the Midlands are often found (*a*) on flat land, (*b*) by a river, (*c*) where there is room for expansion, (*d*) near a coalfield.

The photograph (Fig. 8.3) shows Hams Hall C power station near the River Tame, north of Coleshill. Notice the lines and pylons carrying the power. The production of electricity in England and Wales is in the hands of the C.E.G.B., which divides the country into five regions. Hams Hall is one of the thirty-six stations in the Midlands Region (Fig. 8.4). The stations feed power into a grid (carrying 132,000 volts) and supergrid (carrying 275,000 and 400,000 volts). The C.E.G.B. sells the electricity in bulk to twelve area boards. Each board takes the electricity from the grid into its own network for distribution to the consumer. For example, if you live in Birmingham or the Black Country, your parents will buy their electricity from the M.E.B. (Midlands Electricity Board), which has bought it from the C.E.G.B.

The fuel burned in the year ending 31 March 1970, to generate electricity in the Midlands Region, was:

Coal	26,489,273 tons
Coke	8,386 tons
Oil	375,637 tons
Natural gas	109,784 tons

Coal was by far the most important fuel, and natural gas the newest. Hams Hall C (Fig. 8.3) was the first natural-gas-fired plant in the United Kingdom. It is an experiment by the C.E.G.B. to test the use of natural gas as a source of energy for electricity generation. On 6 April 1971 the switch to gas-firing was made. As a safeguard, if gas supplies fail, the station can change over to coal-firing its boilers, with no effect on its output of electricity to the supergrid.

In the Midlands there is no nuclear power station. A proposal for one at Stourport on the

67

8.3 Hams Hall C power station

8.4 Power stations in the Midland Region of the C.E.G.B.

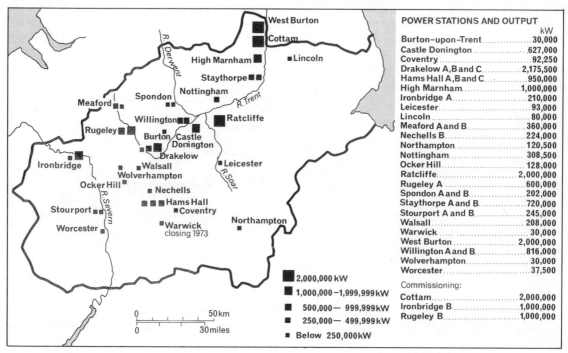

POWER STATIONS AND OUTPUT	
	kW
Burton–upon–Trent	30,000
Castle Donington	627,000
Coventry	92,250
Drakelow A, B and C	2,175,500
Hams Hall A, B and C	950,000
High Marnham	1,000,000
Ironbridge A	210,000
Leicester	93,000
Lincoln	80,000
Meaford A and B	360,000
Nechells B	224,000
Northampton	120,500
Nottingham	308,500
Ocker Hill	128,000
Ratcliffe	2,000,000
Rugeley A	600,000
Spondon A and B	202,000
Staythorpe A and B	720,000
Stourport A and B	245,000
Walsall	208,000
Warwick	30,000
West Burton	2,000,000
Willington A and B	816,000
Wolverhampton	30,000
Worcester	37,500
Commissioning:	
Cottam	2,000,000
Ironbridge B	1,000,000
Rugeley B	1,000,000

Map legend:
- 2,000,000 kW
- 1,000,000 – 1,999,999 kW
- 500,000 – 999,999 kW
- 250,000 – 499,999 kW
- Below 250,000 kW

0   50 km
0   30 miles

River Severn was rejected by the Government. Each region tries to produce enough electricity to satisfy its local demands. Sometimes it is necessary, in order to maintain supplies, to bring in electricity over the national grid from other regions. The Stourport nuclear power station was proposed to help produce the extra electricity needed locally in the 1970s. The risk of danger from radioactivity has meant that nuclear power stations in the past have been well away from built-up areas.

Gas: Coleshill

The natural gas pipeline reaches Coleshill from the East Coast. More than half of Britain's gas comes from the North Sea, although it was discovered only in 1965. At Coleshill some of it is processed and redistributed through the West Midlands (Fig. 8.5). In 1971, one-sixth of all the natural gas received by the gas industry was taken by the West Midlands Gas Board. Natural gas was already in use in England before the discovery of supplies under the North Sea. Since 1964 it

has been shipped in a liquid state from Algeria to Canvey Island on the Thames estuary.

The change in gas production methods in the last ten years is well illustrated by the Coleshill works. In 1952 the West Midlands Gas Board chose a 48-acre (19-hectare) site next to Hams Hall power station to build a Lurgi gas plant. The process uses low-grade coal. The advantages of Coleshill were:

(a) plenty of coal from Kingsbury Colliery,
(b) an existing main-line railway for transporting coal,
(c) supplies of good-quality water,
(d) facilities for disposal of effluent to Minworth sewage plant.

Unfortunately, with the closure of the Kingsbury Colliery and the arrival of natural gas, the

8.5 British Gas Corporation: natural gas pipelines in the West Midlands region (1972). There is a separate grid distributing manufactured gas in the Birmingham – Black Country area, which is not shown on this map

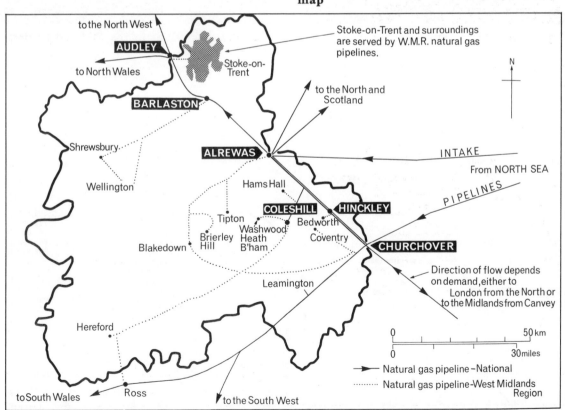

Lurgi process became uneconomic. The works were closed in 1969 and the plant put up for sale. A gas-making plant using an oil gasification process was built on the Coleshill site and produced gas from 1965. Natural gas has now largely replaced the use of coal and oil for gas-making in the West Midlands. This is true of the gas industry in general (Fig. 8.6). One of the biggest jobs created by natural gas is laying the pipelines. Another is converting the gas appliances already in use.

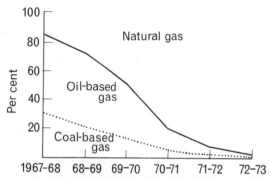

8.6 The replacement of coal- and oil-based gas by natural gas

Oil: Kingsbury

Fig. 8.7 is a press report for 14 November 1971. It highlights the importance of oil as a fuel, and our dependence on the oil tanker drivers, in this case at Kingsbury. Fig. 8.8 shows the route of Britain's first long-distance (245 miles; 394 km) oil pipeline, which was completed in 1969. Midway is the giant terminal at Kingsbury. The pipeline was a joint enterprise by four oil companies, Shell Mex and B.P. Ltd, Petrofina (Great Britain) Ltd, Texaco (Regent Division) Ltd, and the Mobil Oil Company Ltd. Petrol, paraffin, gas oil, derv fuel, aviation fuel and petroleum feedstock flow through the pipeline to the separate terminals of the four companies. Road and rail tankers then transport the products from the storage tanks to customers in the conurbation. The 190-acre (76-hectare) Kingsbury site was chosen for the midway terminal because:

(a) it was on the route of the proposed pipeline;

(b) the land was of low agricultural value;

30,000 pupils hit by strike

Mercury Staff Reporter

MORE than 30,000 children in the Midlands have been told to stay away from school tomorrow because of a strike by 50 oil tanker drivers at the Kingsbury Oil Terminal, near Tamworth.

Schools with oil-fired heating in Solihull and Walsall are the hardest hit by the strike which has disrupted preparations for 11-plus and G.C.E. examinations.

8.7 A press cutting from the *Sunday Mercury*, Birmingham

(c) the area was already semi-industrialised (the Kingsbury Colliery has closed only recently);

(d) there was a railway station and space to extend sidings;

(e) there was room to build houses for employees;

(f) roads could be improved;

(g) it was convenient for distribution to Birmingham and the Black Country.

A second pipeline is being constructed from Milford Haven in South Wales to Kingsbury. Esso, Texaco and Gulf are the three oil companies concerned with this one. The distribution

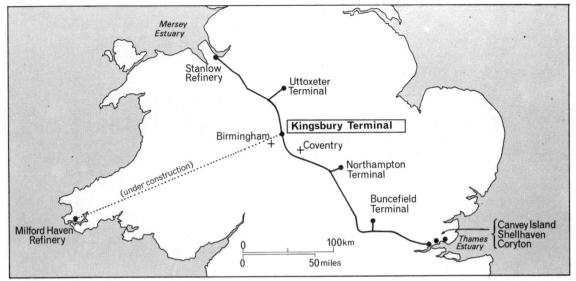

8.8   Oil pipelines

terminals will be at West Bromwich for Gulf, Bromford (Birmingham) for Esso, and Kingsbury for Texaco.

The main uses of oil are for cars and commercial vehicles, central heating, heating processes in industry and as liquid petroleum gas (L.P.G). The chemical industry uses oil products to make plastics, fertilisers, detergents, sprays and medicines.

With the increased supplies of natural gas, the use of oil-based gas has decreased. In 1966, the gas industry used 950,000 tons (965,200 tonnes) of L.P.G.: in 1971 500,000 tons (508,000 tonnes). It is forecast that in 1976 the gas industry will take only 100,000 tons (101,000 tonnes).

Fig. 8.9 shows the various energy undertakings in the Blythe–Tame lowland. Compare Fig. 8.9 with Fig. 8.1 and consider where to place Hams Hall, Kingsbury, Daw Mill and Coleshill on the block diagram. The gas, oil and electricity from this eastern area are all serving Birmingham and the Black Country.

Exercises 1. Use Fig. 8.4 to answer the following: List the power stations (with their outputs) (*a*) along the River Trent, (*b*) along the River Severn, (*c*) on land between the two rivers. Total the output for each of (*a*), (*b*) and (*c*). Suggest reasons why the output at (*a*) is so much higher than (*b*) and (*c*).

Which fuel is used at Hams Hall to generate electricity?

Find out the fuel used at Ironbridge and at Drakelow.

2. From the photograph (Fig. 8.3), draw a sketch to show the cooling towers and the pylons. Use tracing paper as an overlay on the photograph.

3. For what reasons did the Government reject plans for a nuclear power station at Stourport, near the confluence of the River Stour with the River Severn?

4. (*a*) Draw a sketch-map to show the advantages of the site chosen for the Kingsbury oil terminal.

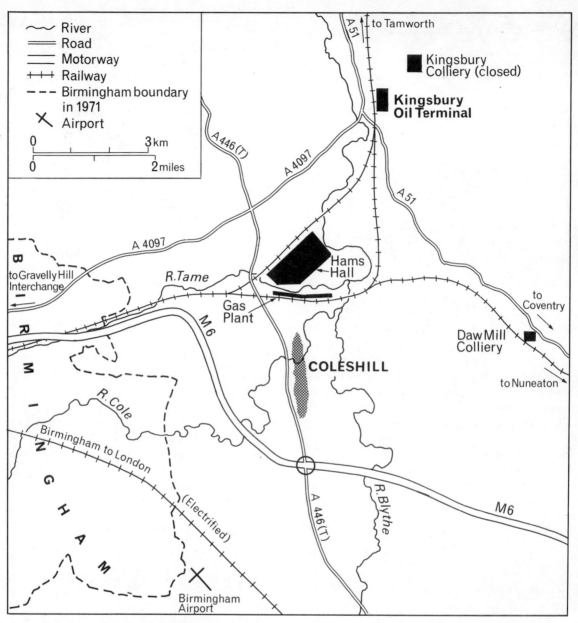

8.9 Energy sources in the Blythe – Tame lowland

(b) Describe one route an oil tanker could take to deliver oil from Kingsbury to Central Birmingham.

5. Gas and oil are carried by pipeline. Where in the Midlands might these pipelines have been made? What else reaches a city by pipeline?

6. Find out about 'town gas'. Describe what has to be done to convert a gas cooker from the use of town gas to natural gas.

7. Start collecting newspaper cuttings on natural gas and oil from the North Sea.

9 | COVENTRY

9.1 Daimler Wagonette (1897)

Fig. 9.1 shows a valuable vintage car, one of a fine set of vehicles held by the City of Coventry Museum. It is the Daimler Wagonette, built in 1897. The Daimler Motor Company, searching for premises to use as a car factory, took over a disused cotton mill bordering the Coventry Canal. In this building, which was renamed 'Motor Mills', the first all-British cars were produced. This was in 1897, and marks the beginning of the motor industry in Coventry. Humber, Singer, Sunbeam, Hillman, Triumph, Standard, Jaguar and Rover were some of the famous car firms which followed Daimler in Coventry.

The present-day car factories are not concentrated in one area, but spread widely over the city (Fig. 9.2). First, there are factories on old-established industrial sites (3, Fig. 9.2). Secondly, large factories (6, Fig. 9.2) were built in the 1920s and 1930s when so many mass-produced cars were in demand. At this time much open farmland was available for factory and housing sites. Thirdly, there are post-war factories (2, Fig. 9.2),

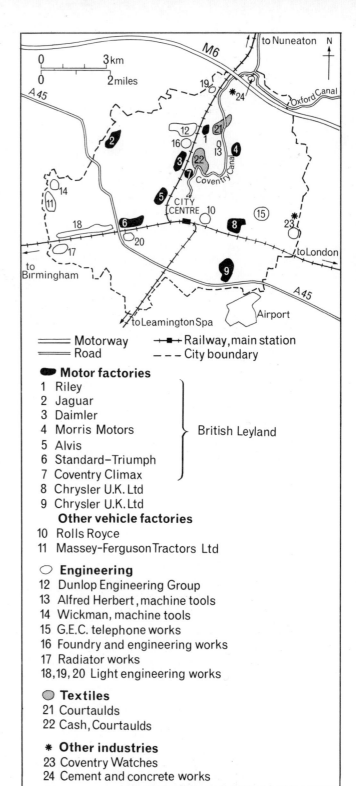

═══ Motorway	─■─ Railway, main station	
═══ Road	- - - City boundary	

⬤ Motor factories
1 Riley ⎫
2 Jaguar ⎪
3 Daimler ⎪
4 Morris Motors ⎬ British Leyland
5 Alvis ⎪
6 Standard–Triumph ⎪
7 Coventry Climax ⎭
8 Chrysler U.K. Ltd
9 Chrysler U.K. Ltd
Other vehicle factories
10 Rolls Royce
11 Massey-Ferguson Tractors Ltd

◯ Engineering
12 Dunlop Engineering Group
13 Alfred Herbert, machine tools
14 Wickman, machine tools
15 G.E.C. telephone works
16 Foundry and engineering works
17 Radiator works
18, 19, 20 Light engineering works

◉ Textiles
21 Courtaulds
22 Cash, Courtaulds

✳ Other industries
23 Coventry Watches
24 Cement and concrete works

9.2 Main industrial areas of Coventry

built on the city boundary bordering the Green Belt.

The car firms are controlled by two large combines:

(i) British Leyland Motor Corporation: the Specialist Car Group – Jaguar, Daimler, Rover, Standard-Triumph.

(ii) Chrysler United Kingdom Ltd: Humber, Hillman, Sunbeam, Singer.

All the car firms except Daimler started as bicycle and motor-cycle manufacturers. Coventry was the original centre of the cycle industry but no bicycle or motor-cycle is made in the city now.

One in every three employees in Coventry helps to produce some kind of vehicle such as a car, van, lorry, tractor or aircraft. Supplying tractors for farm work is a recent industry. Only thirty years ago, horses still pulled the farm implements. Nowadays nearly every farmer has a tractor. Massey–Ferguson (11, Fig. 9.2) is Britain's largest tractor manufacturer. Out of every four tractors made at this Coventry factory, one is sold at home and three are exported.

The parts which go together to make a vehicle are called components. To fashion and assemble these a wide variety of tools is needed. These components and tools are produced in engineering works. Engineering is a major industry in Coventry. Fig. 9.2 shows the location of engineering firms. Number 13 is Alfred Herbert, Europe's largest machine tool manufacturers. The factory still occupies its early site near the canal. Other engineering works (18, Fig. 9.2) adjoin the London-to-Birmingham railway line.

Number 12, Fig. 9.2, is the Dunlop Engineering Group. In 1890 wheels and tyres were produced for cycles and later for the car industry. At a later date, the rubber tyres were made at Fort Dunlop, Birmingham, and the wheels in Coventry. Two major areas of production are steel wheels for motor vehicles and wheels, brakes and anti-skid units in other materials for aircraft. The raw materials for these are brought in by road from elsewhere.

Workers in vehicle and aircraft industries	65,559
Workers in engineering industry	40,754
	106,313

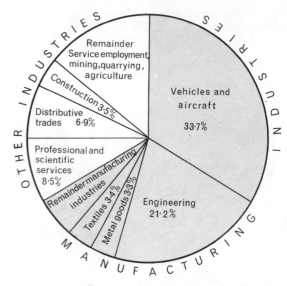

Total employed 191,356

9.3 Insured employees in Coventry (1969)

The total number of workers in Coventry is 191,356.

The sum above tells us that in 1969 the vehicle and engineering industries accounted for over half the workers in Coventry. Closely connected with these two industries are the metal trades. The pie graph, Fig. 9.3, brings out the dependence of Coventry on the vehicle, engineering and metal trades.

Textiles

Although only 6,512 people or 3.4 per cent of the total employed in Coventry work in the textile industry, it is probably the most interesting. Until the eighteenth century, the weaving and finishing of woollen cloth was the chief industry in Coventry, but later silk-weaving replaced wool. The weavers wove silk on handlooms in their own homes. Many weavers' houses remained until quite recently. Fig. 9.4 is a row in the Holyhead Road, 1972. The loom was on the top floor where the large windows let in plenty of light. The local name for this room in a dwelling house is 'top shop'.

The majority of ribbon weavers were independent men who wished to work for themselves. Many settled in new houses with top shops in the Hillfields district. Sometimes a terrace was built by a merchant for his weavers. In these the looms

9.4 Ribbon-weavers' cottages, Holyhead Road

were powered by steam and there was a connecting shaft through the top-floor workshop. This was called a cottage factory. There were also small ribbon factories to which some weavers went to work.

Towards the end of the nineteenth century, increasing competition from French silk firms, strikes by weavers against method of payment, changes in fashion and the increasing use of cotton caused a shortage of work, and ribbon factories closed. It was these empty premises which were taken over by the men starting to build cars.

The two largest textile firms in Coventry are J. & J. Cash Ltd and Courtaulds Ltd (22 and 21, Fig. 9.2).

J. & J. Cash Ltd was started in 1846 by two Quaker brothers who were silk ribbon weavers. A few years later they built a factory in the country, at Kingfield, overlooking the Coventry Canal. Today not only ribbons but nametapes and labels for garments are woven and sent all over the world. There are associated factories in the U.S.A., Canada and Australia. Silk is expensive and the modern fibres used are cotton, Rayon, Nylon and Terylene.

A world without Nylon would seem very strange, yet its discovery was as recent as 1937–8 in America, by Du Pont, the U.S. chemical firm. Nylon is a synthetic fibre made from chemical products derived from coal tar, chemicals or oil. The first Nylon yarn produced in Britain was at Courtaulds in Coventry in 1941. It is strong and hard-wearing. During the process of manufacture fabrics and garments can be set by heat to retain size and shape in wear and wash. Nylon dries quickly and needs no ironing. There is now a variety of synthetic fibres including Celon, Terylene, Courtelle and Teklan. Teklan is flame-resistant and became generally available in 1969.

Samuel Courtauld and Company Ltd was a silk business in Essex at the beginning of the century. It was in 1904 that the firm set up a plant in Coventry to produce the first commercial Rayon in this country. Rayon, or artificial silk as it is sometimes called, is made from a viscose. This is a liquid obtained by treating wood pulp with chemicals. Why a site was chosen in Coventry for this factory was not recorded, but there were certain obvious advantages:

(i) The Coventry silk ribbon industry was declining and men and women used to weaving were available for work in the new factory.

(ii) The Coventry Canal supplied water for the process.

75

(iii) Coal, used as a fuel, was brought by canal from the Warwickshire collieries.

The original factory (22, Fig. 9.2) expanded along the canal bank and to a site further north (21, Fig. 9.2). At first Courtaulds produced Rayon, and later Nylon also, for other firms to weave and manufacture into goods. Now it does all the processes of weaving and knitting the fibre, dyeing, printing and finishing, and manufacturing hosiery and garments. The production is complete from man-made fibre to garment. The Courtaulds Group is made up of 500 factories spread over the world. It has its own chemical plants, wood-pulp factory, packaging, paint and engineering works. The Coventry factories, where all this began, have become the headquarters of the research work and engineering developments.

Points to remember about industry in Coventry

1. The work force is employed by a small number of large firms.
2. Over half the employed people work in the vehicle-manufacturing and engineering industries.
3. Industry is not concentrated in one area, but located in units dispersed over the city.
4. Because factories are in the suburbs, people journey to work across sections of the city rather than into and through the Centre.

Early Coventry

Fig. 9.5 has been drawn from the current 1/10,560 Ordnance Survey map (Map A) to show features of the site of Coventry. An early settlement centred on Broadgate (1). It occupied a spur (C) overlooking the valley of the River Sherbourne. At this point the river has cut a way through a sandstone ridge (A, C, B). The hills (A and B) are the continuation of the spur. By the fourteenth century a walled town (W) had spread over the spur and into the valley immediately below. Ways in and out of the town were controlled by gates in the wall. In medieval times roads were the main means of transporting goods and people. Some roads ran across the country from town to town rather like modern motorways join city to city. Two such roads met at Broadgate

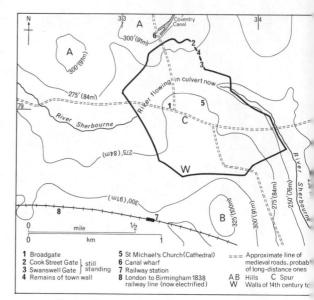

9.5 Some features of the site of Coventry

1 Broadgate
2 Cook Street Gate } still
3 Swanswell Gate } standing
4 Remains of town wall
5 St Michael's Church (Cathedral)
6 Canal wharf
7 Railway station
8 London to Birmingham 1838 railway line (now electrified)
=== Approximate line of medieval roads, probably of long-distance ones
A B Hills   C Spur
W Walls of 14th century to

and their approximate routes are marked on Fig. 9.5. Coventry was therefore a stopping place for long-distance travellers and merchants as well as an important local market town. It grew slowly and by the nineteenth century had spread some way westward along the Sherbourne valley. By then two new forms of transport, canal (6) and railway (7, 8), had reached the edge of Coventry. It was not until the car and textile

9.6 Coventry: boundary extensions

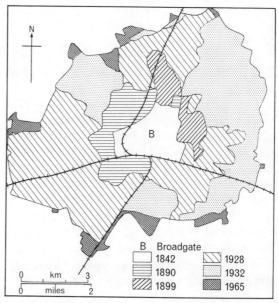

B Broadgate
1842
1890
1899
1928
1932
1965

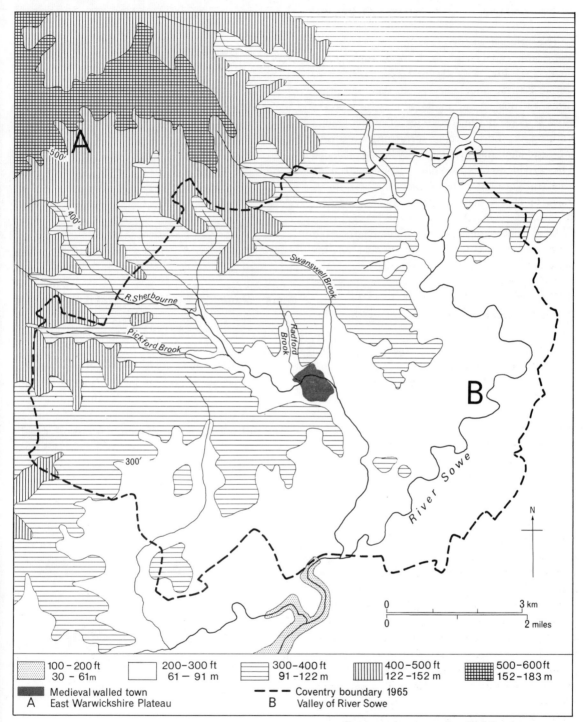

100 – 200 ft   200 – 300 ft   300 – 400 ft   400 – 500 ft   500 – 600 ft
30 – 61 m   61 – 91 m   91 – 122 m   122 – 152 m   152 – 183 m

Medieval walled town   – – – Coventry boundary 1965
A   East Warwickshire Plateau   B   Valley of River Sowe

9.7   Coventry: general relief features

(man-made fibre) industries developed in the twentieth century that buildings sprang up along the canal and beyond the railway. As the boundaries were enlarged (Fig. 9.6), neighbour-ing villages and farmland were absorbed. Coventry in the 1970s has room to build and yet keep some open land. From its small site on a spur overlooking the Sherbourne, it has extended over

77

9.8 Aerial view of Central Coventry (1969)

9.9 Key to Fig. 9.8 (the numbers agree with the key to Fig. 9.10)

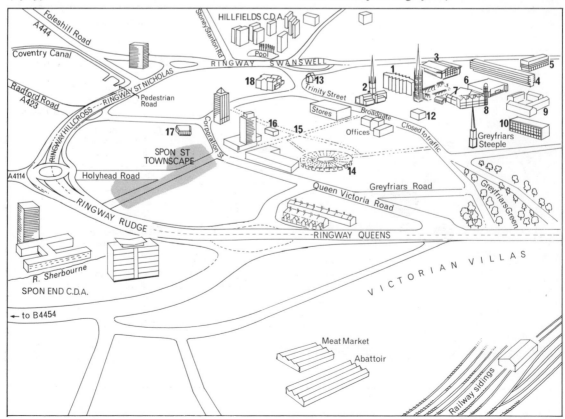

the eastern flank of the East Warwickshire Plateau with its many tributary valleys to the River Sowe, Fig. 9.7.

Central Coventry

Fig. 9.8 is an aerial photograph of the centre of Coventry in 1969. What feature do you notice first? Perhaps it is the wide modern road, or the high-rise flats or the spire of the old cathedral. On the sketch, Fig. 9.9, some of the buildings and roads have been named. Broadgate is an open space laid out with trees and shrubs which were a present from the Dutch people. Around it are department stores, office blocks and a hotel. Broadgate, once the hub of the old city, is the meeting place of areas of the city centre each with its own special function.

To the east is the civic centre made up of administrative, ecclesiastical, educational and cultural buildings. To the west is the commercial centre containing the markets and main shopping precinct. To the north-west is the entertainment centre. All these areas are shown in a simple diagram, Fig. 9.10. The numbers are explained in the key. All the buildings except the Police Headquarters can be located on the photograph (Fig. 9.8). It is possible to identify them by referring to the key sketch (Fig. 9.9) which has similar numbers. For instance number 1 is the cathedral in the ecclesiastical area.

Most of the buildings are new. In November 1940, air raids bombed and destroyed one square mile (2.6 square km) of the centre of Coventry. In the rebuilding, much of the old street pattern disappeared, to be replaced by traffic-free precincts and the ring road. One of the best places to see some of the oldest building alongside the new is at the cathedral. In Fig. 9.11, the walls and tower of the old fourteenth- and fifteenth-century church which remained after the bombing are on the left. To the right is the new cathedral, consecrated in 1962. A high porch joins the two buildings.

Fig. 9.8 brings out the sweep of the post-war ring road around Coventry's Centre. Its route is never more than a half mile (1 km) away from

9.10 Main functions of Central Coventry (use with O.S. Map A)

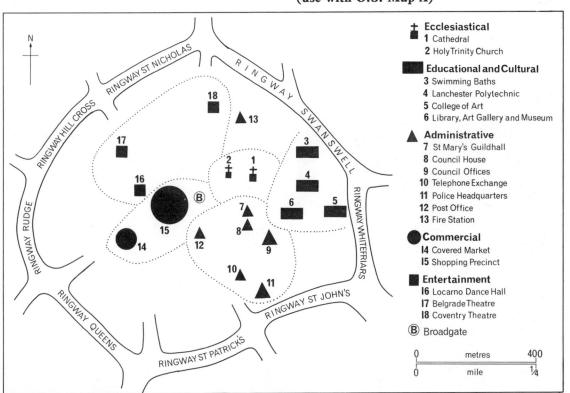

9.11 Coventry Cathedral

9.12 Coventry in 1842 (based on a map by Charles Hansom)

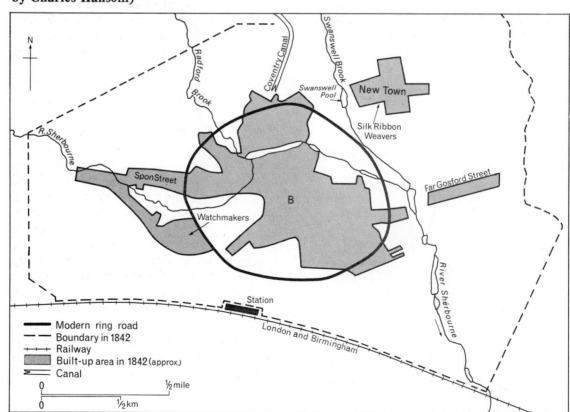

9.13　A timber-framed house

Broadgate. The area of land it encloses is very small. Yet this was almost the size of the early nineteenth-century town. Fig. 9.12 is based on a map of Coventry in 1842, with the modern ring road added. There were even fields as well as buildings within the road's limits. Take a look at 'New Town', being laid out north-east of Swanswell Pool. Later called Hillfields, this was the suburb where the silk weavers were settling.

9.14　The Spon Street Townscape Scheme

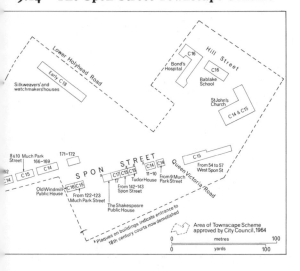

Swanswell Pool is shown at the top of the photograph, Fig. 9.8. Beyond it are nine blocks of flats, part of modern Hillfields, a Comprehensive Development Area (C.D.A.). The C.D.A. is similar to those in Birmingham. There has been wholesale demolition of the old buildings. In their place are the flats together with schools, health centre, shopping centre and land for industry. The silk weaving in Hillfields has died out, and the houses which were the 'New Town' of 1842 have given way to the C.D.A. of the 1970s.

Spon Street Townscape

In the West Midlands, where oak forests were once widespread, the common building material for centuries was wood. A wooden framework was erected, as in Fig. 9.13. The spaces between the timbers were filled with twigs and sticks, then covered with a mixture of straw, dung and mud. This infilling is called wattle and daub. Attacked by the weather, it needed constant renewing and in time was replaced by bricks. The wooden framework varied in style and construction. Up to 1940, hundreds of such houses remained in Coventry. Often the timber frame was hidden by a nineteenth-century casing of brick and plaster. Now, because of war damage and demolition, few are left.

The Spon Street Townscape Scheme (Fig. 9.14), is an effort by the City Council to keep some of these fourteenth- to seventeenth-century buildings. Spon Street lies to the west of Broadgate. It contains many timbered buildings, some already in good order, some worth preserving. The plan is to restore selected existing buildings in Spon Street to their original form; to demolish others and in their place re-erect fine examples from elsewhere in the city. So Spon Street will be a 'special street' of these ancient buildings. Originally they were dwelling houses, possibly with shops or workshops. The intention is to use them as shops. Number 169 is already restored, and number 9 Much Park Street has been re-erected in Spon Street. It is worth noting that the houses chosen were part of medieval Coventry alongside the roads marked on Fig. 9.5.

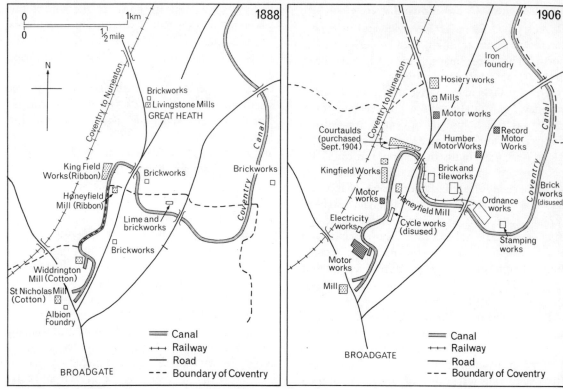

1888

0 [scale] 1km
0 [scale] ½ mile

N

Coventry to Nuneaton

Brickworks
Livingstone Mills
GREAT HEATH

Canal

King Field
Works (Ribbon)
Brickworks
Brickworks

Honeyfield
Mill (Ribbon)

Coventry

Lime and
brickworks

Brickworks

Widdrington
Mill (Cotton)

St Nicholas Mill
(Cotton)

Albion
Foundry

▬▬ Canal
+++ Railway
── Road
--- Boundary of Coventry

BROADGATE

1906

Iron
foundry

Hosiery works

Mills

Motor works

Coventry to Nuneaton

Courtaulds
(purchased
Sept.1904)

Humber
Motor Works

Record
Motor
Works

Canal

Kingfield Works

Brick and
tile works

Brick
works
(disused)

Motor
works

Honeyfield Mill

Ordnance
works

Electricity
works

Cycle works
(disused)

Stamping
works

Motor
works

Mill

▬▬ Canal
+++ Railway
── Road
--- Boundary of Coventry

BROADGATE

1969

Dunlop

Foundry

Alfred
Herbert
(machine tools)

British
Leyland

Coventry Canal

Courtaulds

British
Leyland

G.E.C.

Planned for closure and route to become a road

Kingfield
Works, Cash's

British
Leyland

Ordnance
works

Electricity works

Ringway

▦ Textiles
▨ Motor industry
▤ Engineering
▬▬ Canal
+++ Railway
── Road

9.15 Industries alongside Coventry Canal: 1888, 1906, 1969

The Coventry Canal industrial zone

Coventry had no navigable river, and in 1769 a canal was begun to link it with collieries further north. The three maps, Fig. 9.15, have been drawn from different editions of the 6-inch (1:10,560) O.S. map to give a picture of canal-side development. In 1888 a small section of the canal was still in use in Coventry. Apart from three textile mills and some lime and brick works, there were few industries along the canal. By 1906 modern industry had started. Motor works and Courtaulds' textile factory were established near the canal and Coventry's boundary had been pushed further out. By 1969 the motor and textile industries had taken over more land and engineering had joined them. Because the canal was cut, industries grew up alongside, using at first the coal which was carried. In this way, the canal helped to determine the site of an industrial belt in Coventry. It is a narrow canal around 300 feet (91 m) above sea level. Its terminal wharf ends above the Sherbourne Valley, so avoiding the need for a lock. Apart from supplying water to industry, it is not used commercially but remains a cruiseway.

Although many factories are sited near canal or railway, raw material and finished products are transported in and out of Coventry by road. Delivery of car bodies, engines and components as well as finished cars causes heavy traffic in Coventry from factory to factory. The diagram, Fig. 9.16, shows the basic scheme for a road

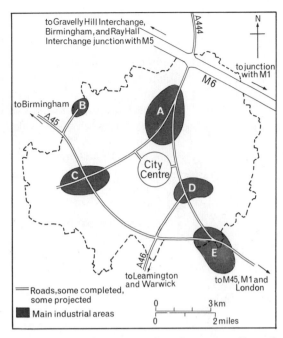

9.16 A road pattern for Coventry (based on *City of Coventry 1966 Review of the Development Plan: Analysis and Statement*)

pattern which would link the industrial areas. This was suggested in 1966 in the Review of Coventry's Development Plan. Part of it has been completed.

Exercises 1. Fig. 9.16 shows the main industrial areas in Coventry. Some of the roads are in use, others are merely proposals.
    (a) List the chief industries at areas A, B, C, D.
    (b) Copy the map.
        (i) Colour in red the roads already in use.
        (ii) Add the Birmingham-to-London and Coventry-to-Nuneaton railway lines.
    (c) The roads have three purposes:
        (i) for people to journey to work;
        (ii) to move goods from one factory to another in Coventry.
        (iii) Suggest a third purpose.

(d) Area E is important for warehouses for industrial firms, e.g. Massey–Ferguson. Can you suggest why these warehouses are necessary?

2. Using Fig. 9.7, describe the site of modern Coventry.

3. Study the aerial photographs of Birmingham and Coventry (Figs. 3.1 and 9.8). Compare (a) the road pattern; (b) the type of buildings.

4. The following topics, which have not been described, could be studied by the whole class working in groups: Watchmaking (Fig. 9.12 shows where the watchmakers were settling in 1842), Lady Godiva, the Lammas Lands, Sir Basil Spence, the industrial Estates, the Town Wall, the airport, the castle.

5. What do you understand by a C.D.A.?

6. In what ways has the City Centre been redeveloped?

7. Coventry Canal is a cruiseway. What does this mean? Which other Midland canals are cruiseways?

8. Look at the pie graphs (Figs. 6.1 and 9.3) showing employment in Birmingham and Coventry.
   (a) Which town has the higher percentage of people employed in manufacturing industry? What reasons can you give for this?
   (b) Complete the following table.

Chief manufacturing industries BIRMINGHAM		Chief manufacturing industries COVENTRY	
1.	%	1.	%
2.	%	2.	%
3.	%	3.	%

Why is the percentage of workers in the metal industries higher in Birmingham than in Coventry?

9. Construct a map based on Ordnance Survey Map A. Copy the grid and number the lines. Add the following, giving a key to any symbols used: Broadgate 334790, cathedral 336791, canal wharf 333796, railway station 332782, railway lines (label these lines correctly (a) electrified Inter-City, (b) goods only), the ring road as completed on this map, Cook Street 335794 (where there is a city gate standing), Market and shopping precinct, Swanswell Pool 333796, Castle Street (Hillfields area) 340797, Greyfriars Green 331786.

10. Write an account of the textile industry in Coventry.

11. At a depth of 2000 feet (610 m) there is coal under Central Coventry. Which coalfield is this? Coal is mined at Keresley Colliery. Where is this?

12. Write an account of communications, past and present, in Coventry.

13. Begin a collection of sketches/photographs/illustrations of different kinds of houses and building materials. Start with an area you know well.

14. It is possible now to walk through the completed timber-framed house (Fig. 9.13). At the Avoncroft Museum (Stoke Prior, Bromsgrove, Worcestershire), more buildings have been brought from different parts of the West Midlands to be re-erected. These include a nailer's workshop and a chain shop. In which town could these have stood originally? Try to obtain a brochure about the museum and visit it.

10 | THE AVON VALLEY

10.1   The Avon Valley

Many people in Birmingham and the Black Country towns like to escape at the week-end to a boat on the River Avon. Hard work by volunteers in clearing and putting locks in order has made the river navigable all the way from Tewkesbury to Stratford-upon-Avon. There are many man-made weirs across the river. A weir holds up a pool of water which can be used to drive a mill wheel for grinding corn. As early as 1660 locks had been built to by-pass the weirs. Before the railway era, wool, coal, grain, slate and bricks were carried along the river. Canals from Warwick (1792–6) and Stratford (1816) linked the Avon with Birmingham. At Tewkesbury the larger boats could pass into the River Severn and out to the Bristol Channel. By the end of the nine-

teenth century, navigation as far as Evesham was poor and above it impossible. The Navigation Trust has worked hard to bring the Avon back into use. There are more boats on the river now than ever before, but they are all pleasure craft.

The River Avon rises outside the West Midlands. It flows 60 miles (96 km) westward to join the River Severn. In its upper reaches it passes through Rugby and to the south of Coventry. This chapter concentrates on the last thirty miles (48 km) of its valley between Warwick and Tewkesbury (Fig. 10.1). To the north lies the Birmingham Plateau, and to the south the Cotswolds. Its chief tributaries are the Sowe, Alne and Arrow on the right bank, and the Leam, Stour and Isbourne on the left bank. The valley is wide but the flood plain is often narrow. It is floored by clay but there are terraces of sand, clay and gravel, remnants of earlier river valleys.

10.2   Prospect Gardens, a small-holding

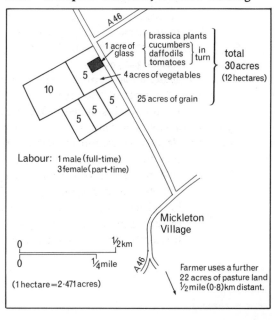

Agriculture

Fig. 10.2 is a map of a small-holding located near the village of Mickleton, south of the River Avon. The farmer grows vegetables and flowers for sale in the Birmingham and Evesham markets. Some of the plants are raised in cold and heated glasshouses, others grow in the open. On the adjoining 25 acres (10 hectares) he grows seed grain, particularly seed barley. About 1 mile (1.6 km) distant from Prospect Gardens he has 22 acres (9 hectares) under pasture for grazing store cattle. In this way he increases his income. Between Bredon Hill and Stratford (Fig. 10.1) the valley is called the Vale of Evesham. It is this Vale, particularly around Evesham and Pershore, which supplies Birmingham and the Black Country with daily vegetables and fruit. Much of the land is cultivated in small patches by separate families working their small-holdings. A family small-holder often farms strips of land some distance apart and of different quality. When giving up any rented land, he has the right to nominate a successor who pays for improvements which have been made and crops not yet harvested. This is called the 'Evesham Custom'. It encourages a farmer to make the best use of his land. The average size of a small-holding used to be 5 to 7 acres (2 to 3 hectares), but at least double this area is now needed to secure a reasonable income. The farming is intensive, that is much labour is employed on each piece of land. The crops are early spring cabbage, salad onions, asparagus, early cauliflowers, peas, beans, lettuce, brussels sprouts, leeks, herbs (sage, thyme and parsley).

Vegetables and fruit are grown on the light soils of the terraces and on the clay lands further away from the river. This farming is called horticulture, which includes:

(a) fruit growing – tree fruits (apples, pears, plums), soft fruits (currants, strawberries, raspberries);
(b) market gardening – growing vegetables (spring cabbage, onions, cauliflowers, leeks, runner beans, asparagus) with some fruit and flowers;
(c) glasshouse production – intensive production under glass of salad vegetables, flowers and fruit;
(d) nursery stock production – growing trees, shrubs and plants for gardens.

The figures in Table 10.1 are based on weather readings taken at Pershore College of Horticulture.

The mild winters and dry, warm springs result in crops being ready earlier than elsewhere in Worcestershire and Warwickshire. The soils of the terraces are warm, well-drained and easily worked. However, the weather and soil are not the only reasons why the Vale has become so important for horticulture. Crops must be sold as well as grown. There is a large population in Birmingham, the Black Country and Coventry which buys the produce. By fast road transport the journey takes only an hour from the Vale of Evesham. The industry is an old one, which became well established over 70 years ago using rail transport. The marketing of the produce is highly organised. There are markets at Pershore and Evesham; co-operative organisations; merchants buying direct from growers; and growers selling their own produce at markets within a 30-mile (48-km) radius of Evesham. The growers are highly skilled and they have been encouraged by local authorities who have provided small-holdings and houses.

Changes are taking place in the industry, such

Table 10.1

	J	F	M	A	M	J	J	A	S	O	N	D
Average rainfall (millimetres)	54.7	34.3	40.9	46.2	59.3	55.0	62.5	73.0	55.8	51.3	61.8	56.7
Average hours of sunshine	49.1	65.4	116.1	136.8	190.9	202.6	186.1	169.3	118.6	99.6	56.3	41.6
Maximum temperature (°C)	11.8	12.3	16.4	19.7	22.7	25.5	27.1	26.1	23.4	19.9	14.8	13.2
Minimum temperature (°C)	−6.7	−4.7	−3.8	−1.3	−1.2	4.4	7.2	6.8	3.8	0.7	−2.5	−5.2

10.3 Aerial view of Fladbury (1947)

as the increasing use of machines for picking sprouts and fruit; a large part of the production is used for canning and processing; people are picking their own vegetables and fruit for deep freezing; there are many more glasshouses, cold and heated; polythene is being used extensively for both low and high 'walk-in' tunnels.

Fladbury

Between Tewkesbury and Warwick over thirty villages and hamlets occur at intervals of 1 to 2 miles (1.6 to 3.2 km) along the River Avon. Map C shows the location of some villages. East of Pershore there are Wyre Piddle (9647), Upper Moore, Lower Moore (9747), Fladbury (9946), to the north, and Wick (9645) and Cropthorne (9944) to the south. The photograph, Fig. 10.3, covers part of the O.S. extract, Map C. The large meander of the river is crossed by a road bridge which joins the villages of Cropthorne (bottom right corner) and Fladbury. A walk through the village of Fladbury from the river bridge to the railway line provides evidence of 1000 years'

occupation. Fig. 10.4 shows some of the features. Finds of flint and pottery suggest that man has probably lived here for 4000 years. Although a small village with a school, public houses, shops and a medieval church, it is changing. The M5 motorway and improved roads have brought it within commuter distance of Birmingham, so people who work in towns like Birmingham and Worcester now live in Fladbury, in new houses which have been built there.

Pershore

Fig. 10.5 is an aerial view of Pershore from which it is possible to pick out some of the features of a market town. With the help of the key sketch, Fig. 10.6, identify:

  the site of the abbey well away from the flood plain;
  the road leading to the river crossing;
  the wide market street, Broad Street;
  the laid-out street, burgage plots and back lane (in Pershore the river bank served as a back lane);

87

mill, weir, lock;

wool barns – evidence of the former wool trade;

modern markets.

Check which of these features can be identified on Map C.

The two churches built so close together need an explanation. Both are medieval churches. Abbey Church was used by people living on land

10.4 A walk through Fladbury

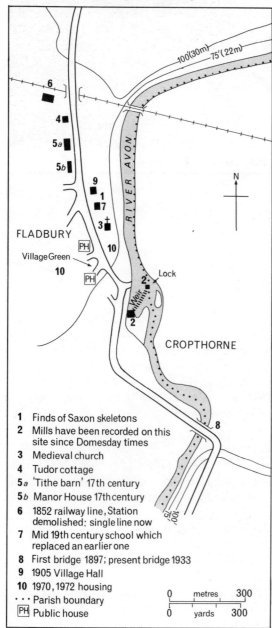

1 Finds of Saxon skeletons
2 Mills have been recorded on this site since Domesday times
3 Medieval church
4 Tudor cottage
5a 'Tithe barn' 17th century
5b Manor House 17th century
6 1852 railway line, Station demolished: single line now
7 Mid 19th century school which replaced an earlier one
8 First bridge 1897; present bridge 1933
9 1905 Village Hall
10 1970, 1972 housing
••• Parish boundary
PH Public house

owned by Pershore Abbey (Fig. 10.6). Land nearer the river belonged to Westminster Abbey, London. The Abbot of Westminster laid out plots of building land around High Street and Bridge Street and erected St Andrew's Church for the tenants. Pershore Abbey is older than Westminster Abbey and its site is marked 1 on Fig. 10.7. The planned medieval town (2, Fig. 10.7) was begun by the Abbot of Westminster. Today Abbey Church is used as the place of worship and St Andrew's has been modernised inside to become a parish centre.

Fine Georgian houses in the main streets reflect Pershore's importance as a market town in the eighteenth century. Wealth came from the wool trade. Wool was collected and stored in barns (Fig. 10.6) until transported along the River Avon. Often the Georgian front to the house hides an older timber-framed building, remains of the earlier medieval town. There are some scattered Victorian buildings, but it is only in the last twenty years that Pershore has begun to expand on a large scale.

Present-day land use around Pershore is fruit-growing (mainly plums) and market gardening. A large proportion of the produce is marketed in Pershore at Pershore Growers' or Central Market Ltd (Fig. 10.6). Some of its produce is pre-packed for firms like Sainsbury's and Marks & Spencer. An industrial estate and a large factory near the railway station are concerned with light engineering. Elsewhere in the town the industries of bacon-curing and flour-milling are connected with agriculture.

Pershore is a small market town with a population of 5,500. For theatres, cinemas and sometimes for shopping, Pershore's people find it necessary to visit Worcester, Cheltenham, Stratford or Birmingham.

Market Towns

Warwick, Stratford, Evesham and Tewkesbury, together with Pershore, form a string of market towns along the River Avon (Fig. 10.1). A market town is a place of trade where farmers from surrounding villages sell surplus goods such as livestock, fruit, grain and vegetables. They also obtain goods and services which the village is too small to provide. The Avon Valley market towns are old ones. Evesham, Pershore and

10.5 Aerial view of Pershore (1966)

10.6 Key to Fig. 10.5

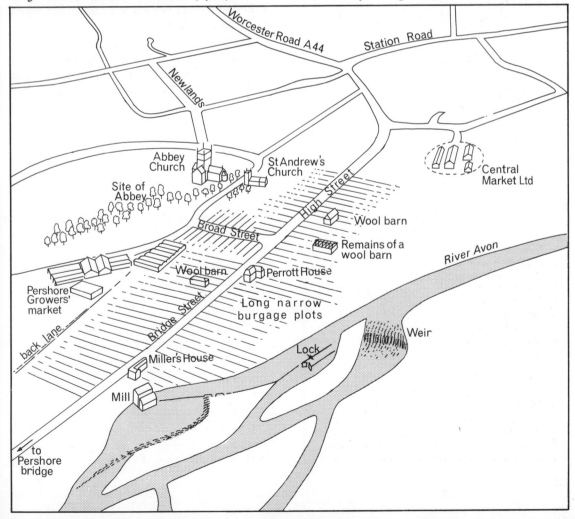

Worcester Road A 44

Station Road

Newlands

Abbey Church

St Andrew's Church

Site of Abbey

High Street

Central Market Ltd

Broad Street

Wool barn

Remains of a wool barn

River Avon

Wool barn

Perrott House

Pershore Growers' market

back lane

Long narrow burgage plots

Bridge Street

Weir

Miller's House

Lock

Mill

to Pershore bridge

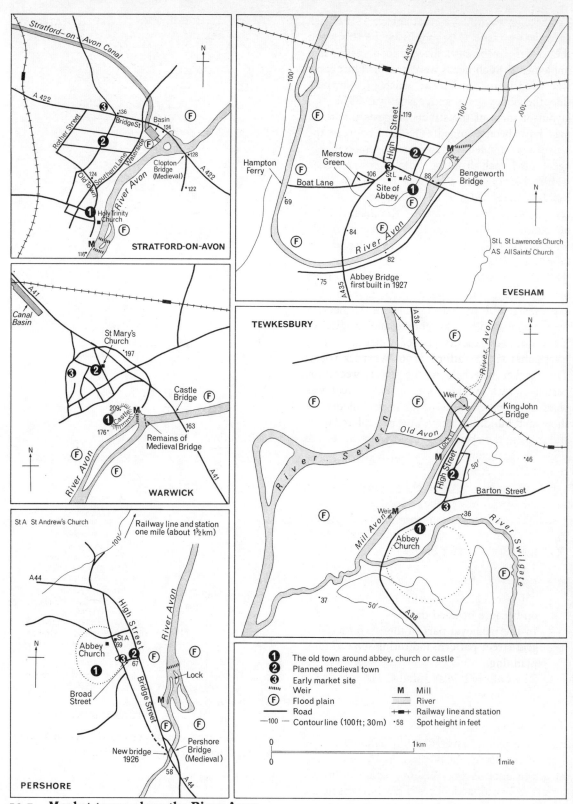

STRATFORD-ON-AVON

Stratford-on-Avon Canal
A 422
③
Rother Street
Bridge St
•136
Basin
124
②
Southern Lane
Waterside
Old town
124
•128
F
Clopton Bridge (Medieval)
River Avon
A 422
•122
①
Holy Trinity Church
F
M
116•
N

EVESHAM

A435
100'
100'
100'
F
•119
High Street
②
M
Hampton Ferry
Merstow Green
106
St L
•AS
88
Bengeworth Bridge
F
Boat Lane
Site of Abbey
①
F
•69
•84
F
River Avon
82
F
N
StL St Lawrence's Church
AS All Saints' Church
•75
A435
Abbey Bridge first built in 1927

WARWICK

A41
Canal Basin
St Mary's Church
•197
③
②
Castle Bridge
F
209•
Castle
M
①
163
176•
Remains of Medieval Bridge
River Avon
A41
F
F
N

TEWKESBURY

A38
River Avon
N
F
F
Weir
King John Bridge
F
Old Avon
River Severn
Lock
•46
M
High Street
50'
②
Barton Street
③
•36
River Swilgate
Mill Avon
Weir M
①
•37
Abbey Church
F
50'
A38

PERSHORE

St A St Andrew's Church
Railway line and station one mile (about 1½ km)
100'
A44
High Street
River Avon
Abbey Church
St A
•69
②
③
67
F
F
①
Lock
Broad Street
Bridge Street
M
F
F
New bridge 1926
Pershore Bridge (Medieval)
58
A44
N

Legend

❶ The old town around abbey, church or castle
❷ Planned medieval town
❸ Early market site
〰️ Weir   M   Mill
Ⓕ Flood plain   River
— Road   Railway line and station
—100— Contour line (100ft; 30m)   •58 Spot height in feet

0   1km
0   1mile

10.7 Market towns along the River Avon

Tewkesbury each had a great abbey. At Warwick there was a castle. The monks in the abbey and the soldiers in the castle needed food, clothes and implements. Such needs were provided by people who lived in the settlement which grew up outside the abbey gate and castle wall. The grid layout of some of the streets suggests that these may have been planned. The land between the streets was divided into long narrow plots (burgage plots), each fronting onto the street. The width of a house on the street was so small that building extended far back into the plot. Entrances were from the front – the main street – or from the back – the back lane. On large-scale maps of Tewkesbury and Pershore such plots can be recognised.

A charter from the King to hold a market brought the privilege of exacting tolls from market traders. This provided an income. So markets were established by the abbots and the Earl of Warwick (Tewkesbury 1086, Pershore 1226, Evesham 1055, Stratford 1196, Warwick 1086.) The market was held in the street, weekly or perhaps twice weekly. The market street was wide. In some cases its width is now hidden by shops and buildings which in time replaced open stalls. From the sketch-maps of the market towns (Fig. 10.7), certain features which they have in common can be picked out:

1. The abbey, castle or church around which the town grew is above flood level.
2. The settlement commands a river bridge. Originally the river would have been forded, then later bridged.
3. The weir and mill show an early use of the river.
4. The stretches of riverine land are not built on because of flood danger.
5. In the medieval part of the town there is a grid street pattern, indicating some kind of planning.
6. The railway line and station are on the edge of the town.

Tourism

Each year more than a quarter of a million people visit Shakespeare's birth-place in Henley Street, Stratford-upon-Avon. Visitors come from all over the world and out of this has arisen the 'Shakespeare Industry'. It takes three forms.

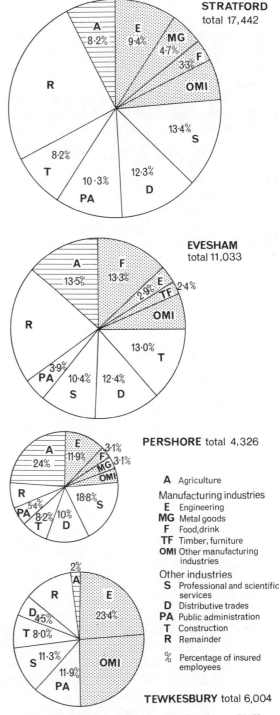

STRATFORD total 17,442

EVESHAM total 11,033

PERSHORE total 4,326

A Agriculture
Manufacturing industries
  E Engineering
  MG Metal goods
  F Food, drink
  TF Timber, furniture
  OMI Other manufacturing industries
Other industries
  S Professional and scientific services
  D Distributive trades
  PA Public administration
  T Construction
  R Remainder
  % Percentage of insured employees

TEWKESBURY total 6,004

10.8 Insured employees in the Avon Valley market towns (1969)

First, provision must be made for the visitors to the Shakespeare Properties, which include his birth-place and the gardens of New Place where he spent his retirement and died. The grammar school he attended, and Holy Trinity Church where he is buried, also attract visitors. Secondly there is the Royal Shakespeare Theatre, where the plays of Shakespeare are performed during a nine-month season held annually from April to December. Thirdly, hotels, cafés and souvenir shops are provided for the tourists and visitors. Stratford is one of the stopping places on package tours through Britain; they bring many overnight foreign tourists.

Industry

The Avon Valley towns are still market centres. Warwick, Stratford and Evesham have weekly cattle markets, and all five towns have markets for vegetable and fruit. As service centres for the neighbouring area, the towns have increased in importance. Over half the people employed are in service industry, i.e. in work connected with the supply of services (Fig. 10.8). Agricultural employment is important in Pershore but not in Tewkesbury. A common industry is engineering, which is related to the motor trade at Stratford, to mining equipment at Tewkesbury, to the making of gears at Pershore and to agricultural machinery at Evesham. Directly connected with agriculture are the canning of vegetables and fruit (Evesham and Stratford), sausage-making (Evesham), ham-curing (Pershore), dairy produce (Stratford) and corn milling (Pershore and Tewkesbury).

Exercises

1. Answer the following questions from Map C.
   (a) Copy the grid and number it. Using the correct symbols, add the river; the contour lines; the churches in Pershore, Wyre Piddle, Wick, Fladbury, Cropthorne; the parish boundary of Fladbury; the orchards.
   (b) For the part of the map between grid lines 98 and 00, look at the contour lines on either side of the river. Compare the slope of the land to the north of the river with that to the south of the river.
   (c) For the parish of Fladbury,
      1. work out its size,
      2. describe its shape,
      3. suggest why it stretches from river to hill.
   (d) Why are most of the orchards on slopes above the valley bottoms?
   (e) Make a list of the different ways of crossing the River Avon, and give the grid reference of one example of each.
   (f) Name (and add grid reference) any village not already named in the chapter.

2. Throughout this book, sketches have been drawn to help identify features on a photograph. Draw such a sketch for Fig. 10.3. It should show the river, roads, railway line, Oxton ditch, Spring Hill, Cropthorne, Fladbury, Lower Moore, orchards, meadowland bordering the river, strip cultivation. (Consult map C.)

3. Using the aerial photographs, Fig. 10.3 and Fig. 10.5, state in what ways Fladbury and Pershore appear to be (a) similar, (b) different.

4. Make a map of a walk through Pershore showing five stopping places which illustrate the development of the town. Number and label the stopping places. The map need not be to scale.

5. Obtain the following for Tewkesbury: 6″ O.S. map SO 83 SW; Aerofilm photograph A 6887. Study the map and photograph and list all the features common to the Avon Valley market towns which you observe.

6. With the use of reference books write about:
   Warwick Castle and the walled town.
   The Severn Ham at Tewkesbury.
   The Grand Union Car ·l.
   The building materials of the abbeys.
   A wealden house.
   Old bridges across the Avon.
   The part played by William Sandys (1636), Judge Perrot (1795) and the Lower Navigation Trust (1950), in making the River Avon navigable.

7. Trace the River Avon from Fig. 10.1. Use the O.S. Sheet 13, The Midlands, quarter-inch series, and add to the tracing all the villages and hamlets between the Avon and the Cotswolds omitted from Fig. 10.1.

8. What is the meaning of the words *bury*, *ton*, *ham*, *ford*, when they occur in a place name?

9. What do you understand by an industrial estate? Describe the one nearest your school.

10. Refer to the weather readings from Pershore College of Horticulture.
    (*a*) Describe the weather experienced in the period of June, July and August.
    (*b*) Which is the sunniest month?
    (*c*) Which is the wettest month? What effect would this have on fruit-growing?
    (*d*) What might result from the low night temperature in May?

11. What differences are there between employment in Coventry (Fig. 9.3) and Stratford-upon-Avon (Fig. 10.8). Explain the differences.

12. The towns of Warwick and Leamington Spa run together and the figures of insured employees are combined. In the pie graph (Fig. 10.9) the letters are the same as in the key for Fig. 10.8, with the addition of V for vehicles and MM for metal manufacture. Using the pie graph and Fig. 10.8, answer the following questions:
    (*a*) In what ways is the pie graph for Tewkesbury similar to the one given here? Can you explain the similarities?
    (*b*) Which manufacturing industry occurs in Warwick and Leamington Spa and not in the towns on Fig. 10.8? In which other town(s) in the West Midlands in this industry important?

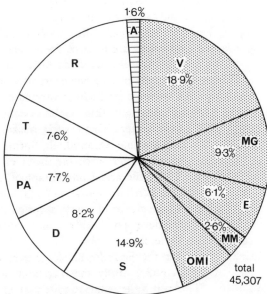

10.9 Insured employees in Warwick and Leamington Spa (1969)

93

11 | THE WEST MIDLANDS IN THE MID 1970s

From 1 April 1974, England was divided into forty-four new counties, six of which are called metropolitan counties. The latter are Tyne and Wear, Merseyside, Greater Manchester, West Yorkshire, South Yorkshire, and the West Midlands, all areas of large industrial towns. Each metropolitan county is sub-divided into county boroughs. Fig. 11.1 shows sub-divisions for the West Midlands. Wolverhampton, Walsall, Dudley, Sandwell (Warley with West Bromwich), Birmingham, Solihull, and Coventry, are the seven county boroughs which together form the West Midlands Metropolitan County. The rest of the West Midlands falls into the counties of Salop (Shropshire), Staffordshire, Warwickshire, and a combined Herefordshire and Worcestershire (Fig. 11.2). Each county will be sub-divided into districts. The changes do not affect the London area, which was re-organised into the Greater London Council and Boroughs in April 1965.

A shop window for Britain

Shortly after leaving Birmingham, a passenger on a London train could catch a glimpse of the notice shown in Fig. 11.3. At present Britain has no large area of exhibition halls where firms can show their goods at Trade Fairs as in Europe. The Government has therefore given permission to Birmingham to build an exhibition centre on a 310-acre (125-hectare) site midway between Birmingham and Coventry. One of the main reasons for choosing this site is the fine air–rail–road communications which exist and can be further improved. The site and communications are shown on Fig. 11.4.

The airport has scheduled domestic and European flights and room for private and charter planes. It is being developed as the regional airport for the West Midlands. A new airport terminal is to be built adjacent to the railway line. The railway crossing the site is the

11.1 West Midlands Metropolitan County (April 1974)

11.2 West Midlands counties (April 1974)

11.3 Site of the National Exhibition Centre, from the railway

Inter-City London–Birmingham–Manchester–Liverpool line. Passenger trains run every half-hour to and from London. A new multiplatform station to be erected on this site will be the first to serve an exhibition centre and airport to be built in England during this century. The road communications will be first-class. The site fronts on to the A45 joining Birmingham and Coventry. Immediately to the north is the M1, M6 link. A new motorway (M42) will skirt it on the east and connect with the M1, M6. Eventually the M90 from Oxford to London will be linked with the M42. Because the National Exhibition Centre (N.E.C.) is outside the built-up area of Birmingham and Coventry, it has been possible to design four special access roads for cars and commercial traffic to junctions with motorways and trunk roads (Fig. 11.4)

The site is in the Green Belt in an attractive setting. An exhibition centre should be near a large centre of population and it is estimated that within a 100-mile (160-km) radius there are 28 million people. The position therefore has been well chosen for quick access to the main industrial zones of England.

An exhibition centre which is purpose-built provides much more than exhibition halls. The firms staging a display need workshops and storage facilities. Conference rooms, shops, offices, banks, hotel, motel and hostel accommodation and car parks must be near the halls. All these are included in the plans for the N.E.C. (Fig. 11.4). Trees, spinneys and hedgerows will be left and a lake constructed to make a pleasant landscape.

At present, developments adjoining the site are restricted in order to preserve the Green Belt. The Trading Estate (Fig. 11.4) north-west of the N.E.C. is to provide warehouses and light industrial premises on land already in industrial use.

One of the criticisms of putting the N.E.C. at Bickenhill rather than near London has been lack of hotel rooms and entertainment. To remedy this, hotels in Birmingham and Coventry are expanding and new ones are being built, and some entertainment facilities will be provided on the site.

The choice of the site for the N.E.C. near Birmingham underlines the importance of the West Midlands in the economy of the country. Birmingham, the Black Country and Coventry form the heart of the chief region for engineering, metal manufacture and vehicle industries. About one-seventh of the national labour force in manufacturing industries is in the West Midlands. In terms of value, more than one-quarter of all new British vehicles roll off assembly lines in the region; machine shops and foundries produce about one-third of the country's metal manufacture. The Machine Tool Trades Association made the first booking for a Trade Fair as soon as the N.E.C. opens.

The site also emphasises Government recognition of the Birmingham area as a centre of national communications. The Gravelly Hill and Ray Hall Interchanges link the M6–M1–M5, and more connecting motorways are proposed. Fast transport for goods to and from the ports is provided through the freightliner depots at Dudley and Birmingham: a key service to European trade now that we are part of the E.E.C. (the common market of the European Economic Community). Although the engineering, metal manufacture and vehicle industries predominate, there are hundreds of associated trades and processes. This great multiplicity of jobs has helped the West Midlands remain a prosperous area. The high density population living in the Birmingham–Black Country conurbation has led to problems of housing, transport and recreational

95

facilities. One question has been how to preserve the Green Belt for farming and recreation, yet provide houses. The problem of transport is acute, because in no other British conurbation does so high a proportion of commuters drive to work. The latest plan is to develop a fast passenger rail service into Central Birmingham from all parts of the West Midlands, re-opening stations and building new ones. By combining bus and rail services into an efficient network people might be encouraged to leave cars at home. The industrial population of the West Midlands provides a huge market for goods and food. One reason for rebuilding Birmingham's wholesale market zone is to cope more easily with the movement of food.

In this book some of the different ways in which local authorities are meeting the problems have been explained. Questions for the future are: how long will the Green Belt between Birmingham and Coventry be preserved once the N.E.C. is built; will the motorways increase the number of commuters into Birmingham and sabotage the moving of people and firms to overspill areas such as Telford and Redditch; will the Government relax restrictions on new industry; how quickly can country parks be created; will the new Metropolitan County Council with its seven boroughs handle the problems more successfully than the local authorities it is replacing?

11.4   National Exhibition Centre (grid reference SP 1983)

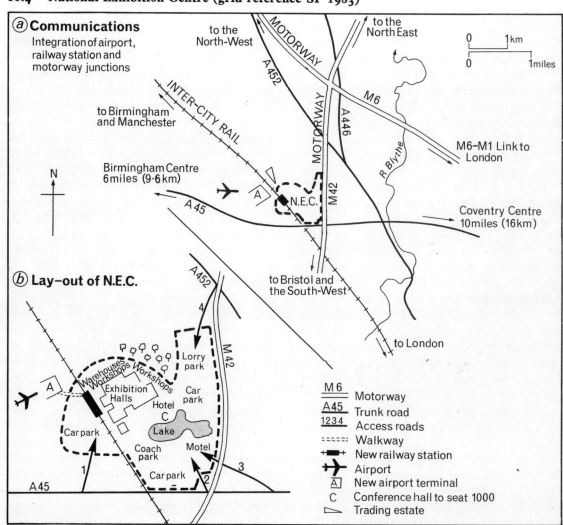